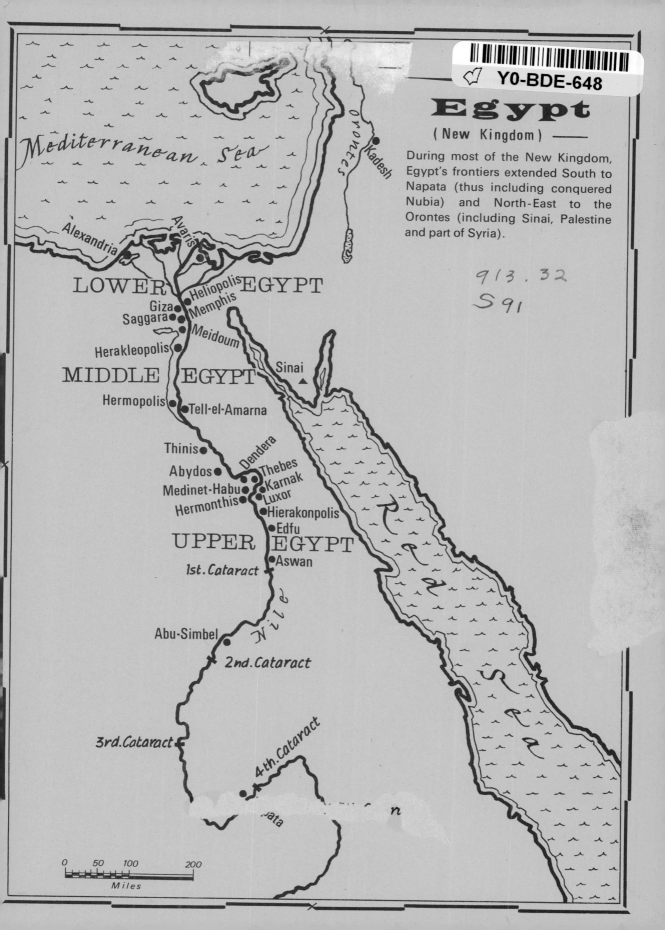

Y0-BDE-648

Egypt

(New Kingdom)

During most of the New Kingdom, Egypt's frontiers extended South to Napata (thus including conquered Nubia) and North-East to the Orontes (including Sinai, Palestine and part of Syria).

913.32
S91

Mediterranean Sea

Kadesh

Orontes

Alexandria

Avaris

LOWER EGYPT

Heliopolis

Giza

Saggara

Memphis

Herakleopolis

Meidoum

MIDDLE EGYPT

Sinai

Hermopolis

Tell-el-Amarna

Thinis

Dendera

Abydos

Thebes

Medinet-Habu

Karnak

Hermonthis

Luxor

Hierakonpolis

Edfu

UPPER EGYPT

Aswan

1st. Cataract

Nile

Abu-Simbel

2nd. Cataract

3rd. Cataract

4th. Cataract

Napata

Red Sea

0   50   100   200
Miles

The Boy Pharaoh
TUTANKHAMEN

Frontispiece : Serket protecting the canopic shrine

The Boy Pharaoh
TUTANKHAMEN

Noel Streatfeild

PILARICA
COLLEGE
LIBRARY

MICHAEL JOSEPH

First published in Great Britain by Michael Joseph Ltd
52 Bedford Square, London, W.C.1
1972

© 1972 by Noel Streatfeild

All Rights Reserved. No part of this publication
may be reproduced, stored in a retrieval system,
or transmitted, in any form or by any means,
electronic, mechanical, photocopying, recording
or otherwise, without the prior permission
of the Copyright owner

7181 0986 4

Photoset and printed in Great Britain
by Westerham Press Limited, Westerham, Kent
in Apollo fourteen on eighteen point
and bound by the Dorstel Press, Harlow

Contents

Acknowledgments

I would like to thank Mrs Stephanie Gee, without whose help this book could never have been written, and Miss Clarissa Barton for the sketches on which the endpaper maps were based. I am also grateful to George Rainbird Ltd, London, for permission to reproduce the colour photographs by F. L. Kenett, and to the following for permission to reproduce various monochrome photographs, maps and drawings: the British Museum, London; J. Allan Cash, London; Madame Desroches-Noblecourt; Egypt Exploration Society, London; the Griffith Institute, Ashmolean Museum, Oxford; the Louvre Museum, Paris; the Metropolitan Museum of Art, New York; Princetown University Press Ltd (Bollingen Foundation); the Radio Times Hulton Picture Library, London; George Rainbird Ltd, London; Rapho Agence Photographique, Paris; Pierre Tétrel, Paris; *The Times*, London. I must apologize to the holders of any copyright which it was not possible to trace.

Bibliography

CYRIL ALDRED: *Akhenaton, Pharaoh of Egypt*, a new study. Thames and Hudson, London, 1968.

HOWARD CARTER: *The Tomb of Tutankhamen* (three volumes). Cassell, London, 1923, 1927, 1933.

C. DESROCHES-NOBLECOURT: *Tutankhamen*. The Connoisseur and Michael Joseph, London, 1963.

The Boy Pharaoh
TUTANKHAMEN

1

What the country was like

In ancient Egypt over three thousand years ago a baby boy was born. He was to be known as Tutankhamen.

It is very easy to think of people centuries before we were born as if they had never lived but were creatures of the imagination, such as Long John Silver or Robinson Crusoe. This is of course nonsense. Tutankhamen was every bit as alive as any baby born today.

Ancient Egypt, at the period now called 'The New Kingdom' which existed around 1500 BC to 1100 BC, does not appear to have been at all a bad place in which to be born. Egypt was at that time reasonably peaceful; it was rich and powerful and immensely old and, as now, the sun nearly always shone out of an incredibly blue sky. The Egyptian people were conservative, liking the old ways, resisting fiercely any change in established customs, so probably there was a feeling of stability, even of contentment.

Prosperity in all hot countries depends largely on water. The ancient Egyptians were lucky because the population

Modern Egyptians carrying water and threshing as ancient Egyptians must have done

(J. Allan Cash)

was sufficiently small for most people to live on the banks of the Nile which over-flowed its banks each year. This meant that on both sides of the river there was fine farming land. On these farms grew grain, some sort of wheat and barley. Vegetables flourished, such as lettuces, pot herbs, cucumbers, radishes, leeks and garlic. There was beautiful fruit including melons, pomegranates and grapes. They had fields of flax from which was woven linen, which was what everyone's clothes were made of, and linen was used also for many domestic purposes. They did not have olive-oil for such domestic purposes as lighting and cooking, but they did have an oil-producing tree though their main supply came from the castor-oil plant and later in The New Kingdom period from sesame seeds.

Another blessing the ancient Egyptians received from the Nile was papyrus. This was a reed which grew pro-fusely in the marshes which bordered the farms. To the ancient Egyptians life without papyrus must have been unthinkable for it was such a useful plant. They cut the pith into thin slices so that it could be pressed together to be used to write on. Royal or rich children used it for their lessons. Boats were made of its reeds. It was also food, for part of the plant was good to eat. It had unlimited domestic uses: things could be wrapped in it, baskets plaited from it, beds sprung on it – in fact it's quite likely the ancient Egyptian housewife might say of papyrus what today's housewives might say of plastic: 'However would I manage without it?'

The ancient Egyptians were also fortunate in their meat, fish and game. The Nile was full of good fish; animals and geese and ducks were farmed but as well wild animals roamed plentifully over the land and waterfowl could be had for the netting. Because of all this abundance ancient Egypt was lucky in another way, its people stayed put. Other races who lived near the Mediterranean and the Red Sea found that after a season or two of farming, owing to lack of water, which meant no replacement of top soil, their land became dust bowls. Because of this they had to move on to become nomads, seeking better land on which to live, and all too often finishing up as slaves.

The Nile over-flowed its banks every year as a matter of course and the ancient Egyptians utilized the water by basin irrigation. What mattered was how high the inundation of the Nile was – too high and it swamped the land, too low and not enough land could be sown with crops – so too well the Egyptians knew what lean years were like.

The ancient Egyptians – an extraordinarily well-organized people – did what they could to guard against famine. They conserved grain. They built large granaries in which were stored a percentage of each year's grain yield.

Anyone who has read the Old Testament will remember the story of Joseph who was sold by his brothers as a slave into Egypt. How he was bought by Potiphar, one of the Pharaoh's captains of the guard. How, to begin with, all went well for Joseph but how later he was thrown into prison where he gained a reputation for interpreting dreams. When, two years later, the Pharaoh had a dream in which seven fat cattle were eaten up by seven thin cattle he was troubled in his mind as to what it meant, so he sent for all the readers of dreams in the country to explain it but nobody could. It was then that the Pharaoh's butler, who had been in prison with Joseph, remembered how he had explained to him the meaning of a dream he had had. So he told Pharaoh, and Pharaoh sent for Joseph who, on hearing what the dream was, told him the explanation of it. There would be seven good prosperous years in Egypt to be followed by seven years of the most ghastly famine.

This dream came true, but by then Joseph, who had become a most important man, had been put in charge of all farming lands, so in every city in Egypt, during the good years, he had stored away grain. This was eaten by the Egyptians in the seven terrible years that followed, and as well there was enough to be bartered for rich goods from neighbouring countries which were also suffering from famine.

Because it was so prosperous most years it might seem that everybody in ancient Egypt was rich and happy. But, of course, this was not true. In those days there was no form of money in general use, so most people would be paid in kind. It was not possible for anybody to take what was not listed as theirs, for the ancient Egyptian scribes

Tutankhamen in the form of the god Anubis   *(Griffith Institute, Ashmolean Museum)*

did a wonderful job stating the ownership of even the smallest field. At the top of the tree the notables would receive huge tracts of land, jewellery, chariots and perhaps horses so that they could live in a stately way. Rather lower down the scale payment would be simpler but certainly would include land. Further down still there might be a tiny strip of land, but more often payment would be in food, coarse linen and perhaps some oil. Right at the bottom were the poorest of the peasants and the slaves. They, too, would be supposed to be given food in exchange for their labour, but too often, if a bad year came, their reward might be reduced to very little or sometimes to nothing at all. Then of course the poor had to beg and steal. So it was no wonder that robbers played a great part in the history of ancient Egypt.

The ancient Egyptians of every class believed that life after death was more important than life in this world. In the very early days the certainty of being reborn belonged only to a Pharaoh. Ordinary men and women, whose great ambition was for an after life where forever they could serve their Pharaoh as they had on earth, could only hope and trust their gods that this could be attained. Because of this universal ambition all houses from the palace of the Pharaoh down to the hut of the poorest peasant or slave were made of nothing more elaborate than Nile mud, straw and some sand, but for their tombs all managed somehow to get the best they could afford.

Bricks for houses were made by kneading mud and

Tutankhamen in the form of the dog Anubis during the course of his transformations

PILARICA
COLLEGE
LIBRARY

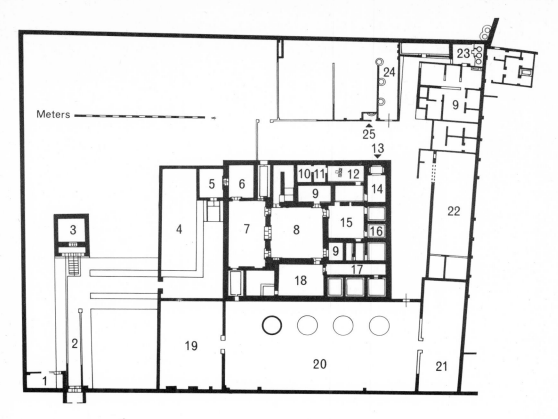

Plan of an Amarnon house belonging to a high official
(Egypt Exploration Society: after Pendlebury)

1. caretaker's lodge	9. store	18. west loggia
2. main entrance	10. lavatories	19. servants' entrance
3. chapel	11. wash room	20. yard and grain
4. courtyard	12. unction room	silos
5. porch	13. recess for the bed	21. stable
6. vestibule	14. principal bedroom	22. servants' quarters
7. entrance hall surmounted	15. harem	23. kitchen
by a loggia	16. nursery	24. cattle
8. central room	17. bedrooms	25. kennel

chopped straw with water, then the mixture was passed to the moulders who, having moulded it, set the bricks to dry in the sun. Being a very hot country the bricks dried quickly, nothing simpler or easier could be imagined. In the palace and perhaps a few houses of the nobles a little stone might be used for show, and cedars might be imported from Lebanon for beams, but generally stone and

The goddess Isis on one of the double doors of the gilt shrine, reminiscent of a chapel of the South

wood as building materials were used only for tombs. The result was houses seldom lasted long for, of course, the bricks broke easily.

A palace or great house, if not intended for a long life, was apparently comfortable.

Palaces and great houses had a high wall round them with one central gate looked after by a watchman. The buildings were usually two-storeyed though they might be one, and almost always had flat roofs where the family could sleep out on hot nights.

Inside the outer wall there was great elegance: pools often full of fish, exquisite gardens and since all the walls would have been mud-plastered, just possibly they could have been painted to suit the taste of the owners for paint is known to have been used inside the houses.

The houses of the rich could be as large as the owners fancied for they possessed plenty of land, though even the rich would have been unwilling to squander good farming land. Poorer people had to make do with smaller houses and the really poor – the peasants and slaves – just managed with a tiny mud-and-straw hut, probably shared by far too many people.

Clothes were very easy in ancient Egypt. They were all made of linen. The rich, both men and women, during the reign of Tutankhamen, for ordinary wear wore one linen garment beautifully pleated which fell from the neck to the ankles, or the man might wear a type of kilt. This linen was often so finely woven it was transparent. They wore

The Nile as it is today   *(Radio Times Hulton Picture Library)*

sandals made of leather and probably a collar, earrings and bracelets of precious stones and beads. This style of linen garment or the kilt was most likely worn also by trades-people and prosperous farmers only the linen would be of coarser weave. Judging by wall paintings the working-man down to the poorest peasant or slave wore just a coarse-linen loin-cloth. All, if they wore anything on their feet, would have sandals made of papyrus. It is probable that, as a very small boy, Tutankhamen wore nothing at all, the Egyptian climate not demanding much in the way

19

of clothing and the ancient Egyptians being not at all prudish about showing their bodies.

Well-to-do ancient Egyptians were fussy about personal cleanliness. They kept their bodies well washed and probably scented. On their heads both men and women wore wigs – the men's heads were shaved. These wigs kept the sun off the head and, of course, as today, meant that the hair always looked just right without continual hairdressing sessions.

Because all the towns and villages lay close to the Nile transport was exceptionally easy. All types of boat transported the people from place to place. Such roads as existed would be mostly dirt tracks so travelling by river was both easier and quicker. It is to be supposed that cattle were sometimes moved by road and ox-drawn sledges could have been used, but the ancient Egyptians were not the inventors of wheels and do not seem to have realized their value, and in any case they were river people so they moved by boat as they always had done.

Pharaohs had, of course, royal barges and though, by the time of The New Kingdom, there were chariots drawn by horses, these were used almost entirely for war or for hunting. Most great processions were on the water.

Nobody can know exactly what the ancient Egyptians believed. Paintings, statues and objects buried in tombs give hints, but that is about all, and no matter how many books you read written by great archaeologists almost none of them will agree with each other. One thing seems to be certain – Pharaohs were accepted as divine. It was because they were gods that in the early days the Pharaohs alone were believed to have the chance of being reborn after death.

At the time of what is now called The New Kingdom, during which Tutankhamen was one of the Pharaohs, this view had broadened out. It was hoped everybody could be reborn, so everybody could therefore expect to serve their Pharaoh for ever and ever.

The ancient Egyptians respected a variety of gods. It is not possible to use the word 'worshipped' because it is doubtful if they knew the meaning of blind, unquestioning faith and love. It would seem there was a lot of magic mixed with their faith, but to upset a god was a risky thing to do so they were careful not to do it. At the same time when tribute was paid to the priests of any god it was probably understood it was for services rendered or to be rendered.

Ancient Egypt from its beginnings in the old Stone Age to the reign of Cleopatra honoured many gods. But by 1350 BC most of the country recognized and gave tribute to only the more important gods. Because of their extraordinary technical feats, such as the incredible pyramids, to build which meant a good knowledge of mathematics, it is easy to think of the ancient Egyptians as advanced in every way. This is quite wrong where worship of gods was concerned for about this they were primitive people. In the early days they worshipped anything different from themselves which they did not understand. In this way an animal, or perhaps a tree or piece of stone, could become a local god and receive tribute as such.

The ancient Egyptians do not appear to have connected their gods with good or evil. For centuries there is not a sign that they had any idea there might be a link between leading a good life here on earth and arriving at the island of the gods, which everybody so earnestly desired to reach. But farther on in their history there are some wall paintings which show a heart being weighed, and this could mean some kind of primitive belief relating the weight of the heart to the amount of good its owner had done in life.

Mummifying was a highly-skilled art which required the removal of all that would decay in the dead body. Nevertheless the Egyptians believed that in some extra-ordinary way the spirit, when it reached the island of the gods, was re-united with the body. At some time after being mummified the spirit started on the difficult and dangerous journey through the underworld – part of which was by water so the dead person's boats or models of them and some oars were buried with them. On arrival, however old or diseased the person might have been when they died, when the body rejoined the spirit it was in the prime of life. As well, those in a position to had little statues buried with them called ushabtis. These were small models of agricultural labourers. The ushabtis were believed to come alive once their master or mistress had reached the island, and from then on for ever they would perform any labour, such as sowing and tilling the fields, for which their master or mistress had been responsible when alive.

The most universally respected of the ancient Egyptian gods was called Osiris. He had a human head. Most primitive people have made up stories to explain how the world began. The Egyptians' story was that to begin with there was no earth, only sea. On the sea there floated an egg or perhaps a flower. Anyway whatever it was that floated, from it the god of the sun was born. This god of the sun became father to four children who between them ruled the world. Two of these children married – for brothers and sisters to marry was a commonplace in ancient Egypt – and they too had four children. They were called Osiris, Isis, Seth and Nepthys.

In course of time Osiris inherited his father's throne from which he governed the world with great goodness and distinction, so he was much loved. The love of the people for Osiris made his brother Seth so deadly jealous that one day he murdered him, then cut him into small pieces which he buried all over Egypt. But Seth had reckoned without Osiris's wife Isis. She, helped by a god called Anubis, collected all the pieces of Osiris together. Of course, though Isis re-animated the body, Osiris was dead so he could not come back to life on earth. Instead he became ruler of the underworld, that underworld through which it was believed all must become part of him on the

Different ushabtis of Tutankhamen (Griffith Institute, Ashmolean Museum)

terrible journey to the island of the gods.

The most important god was Amun. He was the king of all the gods. His headquarters on earth were at Karnak, where he was honoured with great splendour. He was human-headed but was represented by a ram.

The most beautiful-looking god judging by his statues was Anubis. He was represented in tombs for he was

protector of burial grounds. He sometimes looked like a jackal but more often he was modelled as a very handsome dog.

The god who was most important in Tutankhamen's story was Aton. He was the god of the sun. Unlike all the other gods he was never represented except as a disc, though sometimes the rays from the disc finished in small

25

Maize growing in Egypt   *(J. Allan Cash)*

hands. The immediate predecessor of Tutankhamen, called Amenhotep IV, worshipped Aton to the exclusion of all other gods. In fact he so believed in Aton that he tried to force his belief on the whole country. But, as we know, the ancient Egyptians were conservative and stubborn and were not willing to give up their old gods, so during Tutankhamen's reign the absolute worship of Aton passed and the old gods came back into favour. This is a very quick way of telling a large piece of history, for Amenhotep IV was a most interesting man well worth learning about.

Amongst other important gods was Thoth to whom both a dog-headed ape and the ibis were sacred. He was the god of wisdom. A god of which most people have seen representations was Khepri. He appeared as a dung-beetle or scarab. He was made a god because to the ancient Egyptians his ball of dung represented the sun, which they knew was the source of life. When from the dung the young beetles hatched out it seemed to the people like spontaneous life which could happen also to them. Even today it is not possible to go to Egypt without some salesman tempting you to buy a scarab. Not of course that today's scarab has anything to do with the god Khepri, but they are part of Egypt just as leprechauns are part of Ireland.

2

Robbers

The history of ancient Egypt would not have been so fabulous had it not been for her geographical position. She was ideally situated on the banks of the Nile, not only from the farming viewpoint already explained, but because of the natural protection she had on all sides from marauders. To the west she was sheltered by the enormous Libyan desert. To the north was the Mediterranean sea. To the east there was the great eastern desert with, in the north-east, the Sinai desert plus a range of high mountains. There were also cataracts on the rivers, some completely unnavigable, and these prevented a race of warlike people called Nubians, who lived where the Sudan is today, from attacking her. These natural protections were vital to Egypt's development for she could more or less evolve in peace in spite of envious eyes cast on her by her neighbours.

If you look at Egypt's neighbours at the period when Tutankhamen was born you can see how fortunate she was to be protected. Where Turkey is today were the

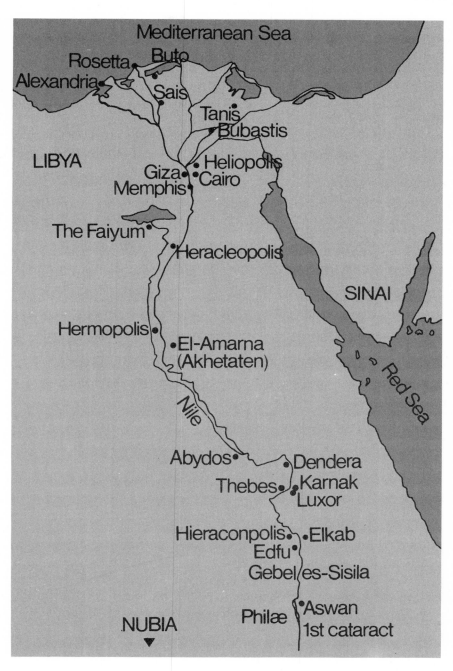

Mediterranean Sea
Rosetta • Buto
Alexandria •
Sais •
Tanis •
• Bubastis
LIBYA
Giza • • Heliopolis
Memphis • • Cairo
The Faiyum •
• Heracleopolis
SINAI
Hermopolis •
• El-Amarna
(Akhetaten)
Nile
Red Sea
Abydos • • Dendera
Thebes • • Karnak
Luxor
Hieraconpolis • • Elkab
Edfu •
Gebel es-Sisila
Philæ • Aswan
1st cataract
NUBIA
▼

Sketch map of Egypt   *(George Rainbird Ltd)*

Hittites – renowned warriors. Below them in part of Syria and Iraq was a country called Mitanni. Beyond Mitanni was Assyria, inhabited by those same Assyrians of which Lord Byron wrote: 'The Assyrian came down like a wolf on the fold.' But, of course, they could not come down like a wolf on the fold of Egypt because she was so well protected.

Other near neighbours were the Kassites who lived where southern Iraq is today, and in Iran there was a race called Elamites. Canaanites lived in what we now call the Lebanon. Syria was where she is today and so was Palestine. Of course with many of these countries Egypt traded, and from time to time she fought them, but on the whole they accepted Egypt as the ruling country and paid tribute to her.

To live in isolation has a tremendous effect on people. Nobody knows exactly when Egypt was first inhabited. She developed through the Stone Age to the emergence of the first small group of farming people, which in time became little townships. Probably the beginning of farming was some type of wheat sown on damp land, and animals would have been kept, but for many centuries hunting both for food and for skins would have been many people's main means of subsistence.

All the same in those early years, so the archaeologists tell us, crafts were growing. The Egyptians worked with flint-tools and with their fingers. They lived in little round mud huts which each family built for itself. They wove both flax and reeds, and they made beautiful pottery. The archaeologists think it was just before 3000 BC that Egypt formed two kingdoms. The country was first separated into nomes or districts, and in time these were grouped together to become two kingdoms – one in the north and one in the south. The chief goddess of the southern kingdom was a vulture and that of the northern was a cobra. The country was unified under the first great Pharaohs and one of their titles was 'King of Upper and Lower Egypt'. So the idea of the two kingdoms was kept even though they were ruled by the same king. The vulture and the cobra protected the king and representations of the cobra were always placed on the front of the Pharaoh's crown. We can see the two goddesses on Tutankhamen's forehead on his coffins. A Pharaoh had different types of crowns but the chief ones were the white crown of Upper Egypt and the red crown of Lower Egypt.

Not very much is known about the earliest Pharaohs. A number of their tombs have been found and they were not pyramids. The first pyramid was built around 2700 BC and this marks the beginning of the period known today as the Old Kingdom. It lasted until about 2200 BC.

The Pharaohs of The Old Kingdom had power which is quite unknown in the world today. Nobody ever questioned anything a Pharaoh said or did. He had power of life or death over all his subjects. All the country was his to do with as he saw fit. The Pharaoh was a god and who

'Sma Tawy', union of the two countries for Ramesses II (Abu Simbel)
('Centre de Documentation sur l'Egypte Ancienne')

would argue with a god? As well he gave the people
sound government with every transaction and law put
down in writing by the scribes.

Head of a 'dummy' of the young Tutankhamen, wearing a compromise
between the crown of the kings of Lower Egypt and the head-dress of
Nefertiti. Stuccoed and painted wood

This absolute rule of the Pharaohs of The Old Kingdom which lasted for about five hundred years did wonders for Egypt. Although to us it seems shocking that so much power should be invested in one man the system at that date worked well. Egypt, essentially an agricultural country, depending on the Nile for its seasonal inundation when farming was impossible, needed state control. During the inundation when farming was impossible, by simply giving an order the entire population could be transported where most needed. This meant they might be used for the building or repairing of dykes, the erection of beautiful shrines and buildings and, of course, the digging of tombs. The flood helped for it transported great blocks of stone nearly up to the tombs. Naturally no special skill was required of that vast labour force, they were just hands to be used as needed. The brains belonged to the upper classes. These, as a rule, were the sons of rulers who had been at school with the reigning Pharaoh, though these too were under the absolute command of the Pharaoh; in return for services rendered they received great gifts, so in time a sort of aristocracy of the intelligentsia grew up round each reigning Pharaoh.

It was at the beginning of the period of The Old Kingdom that a great stone-mason lived. His name was Imhotep. Before he was born tombs of Pharaohs and noblemen were covered with a mud brick top. Under this were the various cells for storing wine, food and belongings which the dead person would need if they completed their

(a) A model of one of pharaoh's boats
(b) The bezel of a ring showing Tutankhamen's veneration of the sun-god

journey through the underworld. At the east end a room was left open for those who wished to bring offerings, and there was an entrance through which the spirit of the dead could slip if he wanted anything.

It was a Pharaoh called Djoser who decided he wanted something rather more modern and more elaborate for his tomb than the usual mud brick affair, which looked like the houses of the period. To design something new he called in Imhotep who had already made a name for himself as a builder. His design consisted of steps which rose up in layers. It was not all done at once, but when it was finished it was 204 feet high. In fact, though small, it was the first pyramid.

Pyramid tombs caught on and as a result the building of the new pyramid-style tombs meant a forward surge in the understanding of stone-cutting tools; it was this that made the building of the great pyramid of Cheops possible.

Naturally these pyramids took many years to construct so often the Pharaoh for whom it was intended was dead and buried before it was completed. What is so fascinating to us today is how they were constructed. As we already know there was a large body of able-bodied men whose services were free, except for food, who could in the seasons when no farming was possible be transported easily and quickly for manual work. But even so how was a pyramid built? The actual collecting of the stone was easy, for this was brought from limestone quarries. The men would have worked with chisels made of hardened

The great pyramid of Cheops   *(J. Allan Cash)*

copper for during The Old Kingdom period there was no iron. Still that does not explain how the stones were put in place; it is all very well to have unlimited free labour, but how do you lift great blocks of stone when you have no lifting tackle? The only answer would seem to be a ramp growing as the pyramid grew, but always narrowing until the peak was reached when it was sealed with a stone cap.

One reason for the building of pyramids, which lasted for another thousand years after the great Cheops was finished, was that it appeared as though they would give the possessions of the Pharaohs protection from robbers. As it turned out nothing the brains of ancient Egypt could invent succeeded in doing that.

Imagine yourself as a poor farmer living anywhere between 2900 and 1100 BC. Inadequately housed in a hut made of Nile mud, straw and sand. Any possessions you had you would have had to make yourself. Probably the wife wove material of coarse flax when she could get hold of any flax. Most likely all the family plaited what they could out of papyrus. For food they ate what they could trap or grow. But remember, when farming was not possible, as for instance when the Nile was inundated, all the able-bodied members of the family would be marched on to boats to be transported to build a pyramid or anything else the Pharaoh wanted, so free time in which to make yourself possessions would have been very scarce. Then a Pharaoh would die and everybody who could by

Procession of the international military guard at el-Amarna
(from 'The Rock Tombs of El-Amarna' by N. de G. Davies)

any means get there would go to watch the immense pageantry of a funeral procession, for all dead Pharaohs were buried with enormous pomp, and even one small object of all the wonderful things of gold and precious stones buried with them would, if swapped, keep a poor peasant in luxury for years.

As a result it was not time, or lack of skilled archaeologists, or centuries of wars that kept knowledge of the ancient Egyptians from the modern world, it was greed, it was robbers.

It is of course a bad thing to be a robber. It was particularly bad in ancient Egypt because the robbers believed absolutely that those objects buried with a Pharaoh were needed by the dead. Once they were united with their spirit, furniture, clothes, chariots, boats, everything they had needed in life they would need again, so to rob them was a crime and the robbers knew it. On the other hand the robbers must have been very brave men. The Pharaohs were gods and facsimiles of the gods were buried with them, so it was beyond imagining what they supposed the form the vengeance of a god might take if they were caught robbing a tomb. On the other hand when you were deadly poor and life stretched ahead of you with one bleak struggling year following another the temptation to rob must have been irresistible. They would either have seen the funeral procession or heard it described, and all that gold and the jewels proved too great a temptation to resist. Anyway, however far from the tomb the entrance was and however carefully hidden, until the discovery of Tutankhamen's tomb – and even that had been slightly robbed – every pyramid and all the later tombs, except one, cut into the rock in what is called 'The Valley of the Kings' where all Pharaohs were buried, were robbed.

3

The discovery

Now we have to skip over three thousand years to arrive at AD 1873 where at Swaffham in Norfolk the man was born who found the tomb of Tutankhamen. His name was Howard Carter.

In everybody's life chance plays a big part. Home influences, school influences, even what may seem a casual meeting and the mind or the imagination is stirred, and off we sail in some quite different direction from the one that had seemed planned for us. In Howard Carter's childhood two factors influenced especially his future life. The first was that his father was an artist. In the last century it was quite usual for people with money to have portraits painted of their animals. Plenty of such portraits can be seen today: race-horses, hunters, dogs of every size and shape, bulls – all and every animal of which the owner was fond or proud. Howard Carter's father was an animal artist so he was constantly away painting his sitters or, more correctly, his standers.

It often happens that a parent's gift is passed on to a child in a slightly different form. This happened to Howard. He had an artist's eye and an artist's fingers, and both were to shape his future career. Another factor – and a very important one – was his education. Owing to the fact that he was delicate he was not sent to school but was educated at home. This probably meant a tutor for a few hours a day and some homework, but it would also mean many hours of leisure to do with what he liked. There does not appear to have been any interest in archaeology in his schoolboy years, but there was an interest in meticulous copying, especially of lettering, and it was this gift which first took him to Egypt.

It was in 1892 that Howard was first invited to go to Egypt to copy the inscription on a tomb. That first visit settled the shape his life would take, he came back a dedicated Egyptologist and never wished to be anything else. An archaeologist, however enthusiastic, cannot dig just where he fancies. Archaeology is immensely expensive so there must be a backer who provides the money. In 1902 the money was provided by a rich enthusiast, an American called Theodore Davis who held a concession from the Egyptian government to dig in The Valley of the Kings where, as already stated, all the Pharaohs were buried. In 1903 Howard Carter, by then an established Egyptologist, was employed by Theodore Davis and helped in the discovery of many important finds.

Dedicated Egyptologist that he was, what Howard

ABOVE *Portrait of Lord Carnarvon as a young man*
BELOW *Howard Carter at the time of the discovery*
(Radio Times Hulton Picture Library)

wanted was to have his own dig. He was enthralled by The Valley of the Kings, and he dreamed of a day when he would not dig to another man's orders but decide for himself where possible finds lay. In 1907 Howard Carter's dream began to come true. He found a patron, his name, which was to become famous, was George Edward Stanhope Molyneux Herbert afterwards 5th Earl of Carnarvon.

No two boys could have had more dissimilar backgrounds. Lord Carnarvon, or Lord Porchester as he then was, in 1866 was born into an enormously rich family. He was educated at a private school, then at Eton, and was then sent to Trinity College, Cambridge.

Lord Carnarvon was an exceptionally gifted man. He was a real connoisseur of the arts. His special subject was history and he became an ardent amateur Egyptologist. He was also a sportsman.

It was ill-health that brought Lord Carnarvon to Egypt. He had one of the earliest cars ever seen on the roads. One winter when driving in Germany he met with an accident and, though he recovered from it, he had very bad health for the rest of his life, including weak lungs. It was his weak lungs that took him to the blue skies and blazing sun of Egypt where in 1907 he was first introduced to Howard Carter.

This is a good place to think about the curse of the Pharaohs – the legend that has always hung around that ill-luck comes to those who dig up dead Pharaohs. Lord

Carnarvon is considered the proof of this legend for he met with a fairly sudden end soon after Tutankhamen's tomb was opened. What happened was he got a bad mosquito bite which turned septic (it was, remember, years before the discovery of penicillin) and from this he developed pneumonia which killed him. Against this Howard Carter who, had there been a word of truth in the story of the curse of the Pharaohs, must have been the number one offender lived to be well on in his sixties. But two other members of the team of diggers also died, so the story grew and is still widely believed. There were two odd things that did happen at the time of Lord Carnarvon's death in April 1923 which added fuel to the fire. The first was that the moment Lord Carnarvon died in Cairo inexplicably every light in the town went out. The second odd thing was about his son's dog. The son, then Lord Porchester who was serving with the army in India, had left the dog in Hampshire in his father's charge and it had become devoted to him. At the exact moment when Lord Carnarvon died this dog began to howl and went on howling until it too died. All very strange, even uncanny, but surely nobody can really imagine that the deaths or the peculiar occurrences had anything to do with the long-dead Tutankhamen.

The relationship between Lord Carnarvon and Howard Carter cannot have been an easy one. Both were temperamental and both self-willed. There were also differences in outlook. Lord Carnarvon felt that as he was spending a vast fortune on his search for knowledge of ancient Egypt, what was found if anything was of value should be sold to him. Howard Carter, on the other hand, equally dedicated in his search for knowledge, believed that all that was found should stay in Egypt, the property of the Egyptian government. What is known is that however many arguments there may have been in private, in public they worked together without too much friction. Howard Carter with an army of assistants digging, on the left bank of the Nile, exploring the western part of Thebes, the known capital of most of the Pharaohs, and Lord Carnarvon in Egypt whenever possible, always paying the vast wages bills.

In 1912 Howard Carter decided to dig in a new area. He selected the neighbourhood of a place called Sais. But he and his fellow-workers were quite literally chased out of that neighbourhood by hordes of cobras. It must be a tough life being an Egyptologist.

Just before the first world war Howard Carter was back digging around Thebes. But when the war started his work of course slowed right down. He remained in Egypt because he was conscripted there. Lord Carnarvon, far too delicate for war service, was however unable to get to Egypt again until the war finished. But by 1919 they were working together once more, and they continued digging, except in the very hot weather, until 1921.

All through these years Howard Carter had found hints of a little-known Pharaoh. As far as the ancient world

ABOVE *Howard Carter and Lord Carnarvon in Egypt*
BELOW *The site of Tutankhamen's tomb, with the Valley of Kings in the background*

(Radio Times Hulton Picture Library)

was concerned there had never been such a person as Tutankhamen for immense trouble had been taken by his successors to see that his name was erased from Egyptian history. All the same, in spite of his faith in this Pharaoh, in 1922 Howard Carter suddenly lost heart. So much digging and so little in terms of history to show for it. As well Lord Carnarvon's permit to dig was running out, there were only a few more weeks to go. Then on the morning of November 4th 1922 the great break-through occurred. Howard Carter went to the dig to be greeted by a strange silence. Where he had been digging he saw the beginning of a stone step. This step was followed by others and then came a screen of stones covered in plaster which had on it seals belonging to a royal tomb.

There were in all sixteen steps to be cleared, and then they came to the last barrier between themselves and the burial place. On this was the name Nebkheprure-Tutankhamen.

Howard Carter went no further. He sent a cable to Lord Carnarvon, and he and his daughter arrived at the tomb on November 26th. It was then that Howard Carter pulled out some stones and inserted his torch. Its light revealed a room glittering with gold.

In that second three men achieved everlasting fame. Howard Carter, Lord Carnarvon and the so far totally unknown Pharaoh, Tutankhamen.

4

Tutankhamen the baby

Nobody knows who Tutankhamen's father and mother were. Nobody knows where he was born, or for certain who brought him up, but roughly they know what date he lived. He belonged to that period called today The New Kingdom.

Thebes, as we know, had since the beginning of the period been the capital of the Pharaoh. Here they had their greatest palaces; here all the contemporaries of the Pharaoh, who would be his men in office, lived, as did the courtiers, high army and state officials. Here also was Karnak, the centre of the worship of the god Amun.

The first Pharaoh to rebel against the supremacy of Karnak was the father of the Pharaoh who perhaps brought Tutankhamen up, he was called Amenhotep III. Amenhotep resented the enormous influence exerted by the priests of Karnak, for he had a deep admiration for the god of the sun Aton. Much of this troubled history is lost in the mists of time and anyway there is a lot of argument

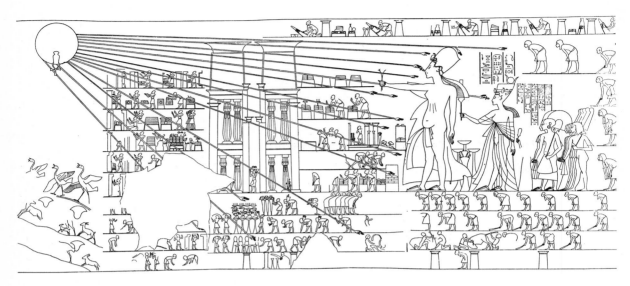

Worship of the rising sun in the royal tomb of el-Amarna
(Monuments for the study of the Cult of Atonou in Egypt)

about what happened, but that there was a determination on the Pharaoh's part to reduce the power of Karnak during his reign seems likely, and it is quite certain that it was in this atmosphere that his son Amenhotep IV was reared.

Amenhotep IV seems to have been in every way a most unusual man. To look at he was hideous. According to some Egyptologists he had an elongated head which sagged forward, a very ill-shaped nose and thick lips and a thin weedy body with scraggy legs. Yet in this misshapen body there was a fine brain and terrific character. He did not just wish to reduce the power of Karnak, he utterly rejected it and all gods except the one god Aton. This, as an individual opinion, would not have been so horrifying

Tutankhamen on a papyrus raft, in the attitude of a harpooner. One of the funerary objects used to evoke the mystical pilgrimages during the funeral. Gilded wood

to the Egyptians but he insisted that they should feel as he did. In Amenhotep IV's case the word 'worshipped' seems fitting for it would appear that he had the dawning of an idea of what blind unquestioning faith and love might mean.

It is easy to imagine as his reign continued with what fear many of the ancient Egyptians viewed Amenhotep IV. Conservative as they were they did of course honour, respect and in their fashion worship their Pharaoh. But what about Amun? What about the other gods? The people's allegiance must literally have been torn apart.

Amenhotep IV must have caused havoc in Thebes. He had removed from temples and royal statues every hieroglyphic that meant Amun. He changed his own name to Akhenaton, which meant the spirit of Aton. He persecuted the priests of Karnak, cutting off from them all the rich offerings which by tradition had flowed to them from the reigning Pharaoh. He forbade the worship of Amun in any temple. In fact in many ways he brought the busy, bustling life of Thebes to a standstill.

Mind you, although Akhenaton was a bigot as is anybody who believes that all must believe what they believe, there was right on his side. Over the years the priests of Amun, hoping to squeeze more money out of the faithful, had fostered a reign of terror. They had invented the most shocking list of ghastly monsters and demons which they preached haunted that island of the gods which they all hoped their spirits would some day reach.

The king wearing the red crown of the North and holding the royal insignia.
One of the funerary objects used to evoke the mystical pilgrimages during
the funeral

The only way, the priests had stated, to exorcise these evil creatures was by gifts to Amun, and by gifts they meant big gifts, so they had extorted everything that could be squeezed out of the long-suffering people.

After five years of trying to force Aton on Thebes and obliterate Amun, Akhenaton decided he would be easier in his mind and spirit in a new town given entirely to the worship of Aton. So he moved north. He chose a beautiful site between where Cairo is now and Luxor. That town is now called el-Amarna.

It was in el-Amarna that somewhere around the year 1350 Tutankhamen was born. Although nobody knows who his father and mother were he was apparently accepted as a royal relative, so there would of course have been great rejoicings at his birth. As a semi-royal baby in a land full of slaves little Tutankhamen would have had a vast number of servants to wait on him from the moment he was born. No doubt a head-nurse, she would probably have been high born, but under her there would have been many nursery-maids. There would have been a staff in charge of the royal nurseries and of course specialists of various kinds to make sure all was well with the little boy.

But Tutankhamen was probably not dependent on his staff for loving care. Akhenaton was married to a most beautiful queen called Nefertiti. Akhenaton and Nefertiti had six daughters but no sons so, of course, the family would be delighted to have a baby boy to make a fuss of,

Akhenaton and Nefertiti   *(Louvre Museum, photo Pierre Tétrel)*

so the chances are he was brought up with the princesses in the royal palace.

From wall paintings the Egyptologists deduce that Akhenaton and Nefertiti and their little girls had for some years a happy home life. Akhenaton was evidently what is known as a family man for he seems to have enjoyed having his wife and family with him. It can also be imagined that el-Amarna was a pleasant place in which to live, for no doubt Akhenaton and his friends and advisors would have planned a town with all the beauty of Thebes only improved by more up-to-date amenities though it was not famous for good workmanship. Probably it had wide roads and beautiful palaces, though the town was built in far too much of a hurry. It certainly had fine temples to the glory of Aton, and no doubt splendid residences for his priests. Any new town in Egypt would have glowed and shone under the glorious blue sky, and where the well-to-do lived there would have been flowers everywhere in formally laid-out gardens, and of course ornamental lakes with beautiful birds swimming on them.

At this time when Tutankhamen was born the third of the six princesses would have been perhaps two or three. Her name was Ankhesenpaton and, of course, like all little girls, she would have loved a doll or its equivalent and it is likely she considered the baby boy her special doll. She would have helped him to walk and even, when he could barely toddle, would have taken his hand and showed him all the wonders of the palace gardens. There is nothing that the Egyptologists have discovered to suggest what as babies those two called each other, but common sense tells us that no baby boy of any date could get his tongue round a name like Ankhesenpaton, and she would probably have had great difficulty in saying Tutankhamen, so possibly they called each other Ank and Tut, but we shall never know so we have to use their names in full.

Rich children in ancient Egypt were not short of toys. No doubt the poor child gave its love to a strip of papyrus wrapped in a linen rag, or a piece of drift-wood shaped like a horse, but for those who could pay or barter there were splendid toys, especially models of animals, some of which had movable limbs.

It was of course usually hot in el-Amarna so you can picture Tutankhamen clutching Ankhesenpaton's hand toddling round naked, probably accompanied by an assortment of family pets. The ancient Egyptians were animal lovers. The family animals in Tutankhamen's day possibly included greyhounds and some say little dogs called ketkets. There would have been a big assortment of household cats, some monkeys, perhaps apes and probably a few pet birds.

Baby days pass quickly so it is a likely guess that by the time Tutankhamen was four his education would have started. His school would probably have been held in the palace, and children of family friends of his age would have been invited to work with him. For school he would probably have said good-bye to running about with no clothes on but would have worn a loin-cloth held in place by a belt, and he might even have been made to wear sandals. Ankhesenpaton, who would have started lessons before Tutankhamen, would have worn the fine linen pleated dress shown in so many wall paintings.

Tutankhamen when very young. Figures on walking sticks, one of gold and one of silver   *(Griffith Institute, Ashmolean Museum)*

Most lessons one would guess would be taught by the priests or scribes. The priests would of course be the priests of Aton whom both children, especially the princess, would have been brought up to honour as the one true god. The first lessons, like first lessons everywhere, would be how to read and how to write.

To attend school Tutankhamen would have been equipped like a little scribe. No doubt like any little boy today carrying his first satchel or wearing a first school cap, he would have been enormously proud of himself. He would have carried a palette. This was a board, probably in his case made of valuable material, perhaps ivory or even possibly gold. In this board were two hollows to hold the then equivalent of ink. They were solid blocks, one black and one red; they were made of ochre mixed with gum. For pens the children used small water reeds chewed at one end into a sort of paint brush. These reeds were of course very fragile so there was a hollow in the board in which they were kept, rather as children today use a pencil-box.

Seeing who he was Tutankhamen would have learnt to write on papyrus; poorer children, if they learnt to write at all, would have used broken pieces of coarse pottery, but papyrus was valuable so Tutankhamen had some-

Tutankhamen's ivory 'papyrus smoother'   (*Griffith Institute, Ashmolean Museum*)

thing he could use as an indiarubber to get rid of his mistakes. This was a scraper made of fine sandstone which he would have kept in a little leather bag with a draw-string top. As well he would have had a small sponge for washing away either mistakes or the day's work, for papyrus in schools seems to have been used rather as children in the last century used a slate. As well of course he had to have a bowl of water into which he dipped his brush before using his colour block. He would work from the black block; corrections by his teachers were made in red.

Learning to write in ancient Egypt was a mammoth task for all children, and it would have been particularly hard for Tutankhamen because with his connection with the royal family he would be expected to do better at lessons than the rest of the school.

Writing was rather like Chinese writing today; it was done with a series of hundreds of pictures. That is to say, if he were writing about the god Aton he drew him in a special way which was recognized by all who could read. If he wanted to say somebody travelled by boat he drew a boat, not any old boat but the boat the scribes had over the years decided was the right emblem for a boat. There was not naturally any connection at all between what was written in pictures and the sound used when the picture was described in words. The mind boggles at the thought of what it could have been like for Tutankhamen and his fellow students, who had to learn by heart the endless symbols to be drawn for every single thing a scribe might need to put on paper. This sort of writing we call 'hieroglyphic'.

There was a slightly simpler way of writing which we call 'hieratic'. It was a quicker way of writing because the drawings were simplified, and so it was possible to go on writing in a more or less steady flow as we do today, without the necessity of filling the reed brush with more colour before every drawing. There seems nothing to prove it, but at a guess it seems likely Tutankhamen learnt hieratic writing, for by the time he was growing up it was always used on papyrus by the scribes in the day-to-day running of the state.

The ancient Egyptians though they had no alphabet had a calendar. This was based on study of the stars. Naturally this had over the years been built on a study of seasons, particularly on the behaviour of the Nile, but it was a good calendar not unlike our own. Of course Tutankhamen would have had to learn all about it as one of his lessons. To the priests the calendar was of incalculable value in handling the uneducated, because such people believed that the priests' knowledge in advance of how the Nile was going to behave must have given the impression that they could control it. If you come to think of it this is not unlike the way in which some people expect the TV weather forecasters to control our weather.

Other subjects Tutankhamen might have had to study were mathematics, geometry and a foreign language, probably Akkadian, which was the diplomatic language of the time. The ancient Egyptians were a practical people, they did not seek knowledge for the sake of knowledge, they wanted it only for special purposes. Years before Tutankhamen was thought of they had been forced to work out how many vast stones they would require to build a pyramid, how many stones would be needed to put back boundaries lost in a flood. They seem to have counted from one to ten only, and after that they used some sort of abacus. Mostly figures would be used only by scribes, but it is unlikely that Tutankhamen would not have been taught the meaning of them.

In the afternoons the children had physical exercise. Tutankhamen would have learnt how to wrestle, archery and how to drive a chariot. The master-at-arms would have taught him to hunt. He just might have been taught to ride as Akhenaton owned many thoroughbred horses presented to him by neighbouring states, but horse riding was unusual in ancient Egypt where horses were kept to pull chariots.

The princess Ankhesenpaton, though she probably learnt to wrestle – it would have been considered good for the figure – spent her afternoons at more female occupations. She played ball-games, also good for the figure, she learnt to dance and to juggle and she would have studied music – most likely the harp.

It is probable the two children, just like children of any date, liked best of all their leisure time. Then they could

Tutankhamen's 'lighter'   *(Griffith Institute, Ashmolean Museum)*

do what they wanted, amuse themselves together in the garden or perhaps sit on the floor indoors and play games. A favourite game of the period was played with dice and pieces not unlike draughts. Tutankhamen was also very fond of playing with a toy which made sparks fly, in fact a type of lighter. He was so fond of this that it was buried with him.

Even while they were quite small the two children may have clung to each other. They could have been conscious in the half-understood way that children of all dates have felt when there is trouble around them, that things were going wrong in their home. If this were to happen the quiet happiness to which they were used might be coming to an end and they, poor mites, like dandelion seeds, blown by a wind, would have no more power than today's children to decide where they would end up.

59

5

The coronation

The troubles the children may have felt hanging over them were very real. Akhenaton's passion for the god Aton would seem as the years passed to have grown out of all proportion. Indeed towards the end of his life as he got more and more ill he cared almost entirely for his temple duties, and nothing at all about what was happening in his own country or in the neighbouring countries.

Some changes must have been obvious even to Tutankhamen, young as he was. When he was a little boy he would have seen and been part of great processions when the satellite countries brought rich tribute to Akhenaton. But as the Pharaoh ceased to care what happened outside el-Amarna the news of course spread and very little tribute arrived. Indeed many of the satellite countries ceased to pay even lip service to Egypt but formed other alliances. Days when tribute arrived would have been days of public rejoicing, so would have been fun for the children and they would have missed them

Detail from the processions and celebrations of the Nubians during the
'Parade of foreign tribute' in the year 12
(from 'The Rock Tombs of El-Amarna' by N. de G. Davies)

when they stopped.

Egypt had always been a country needing good strong
government and she had usually had it. Now, with a sick
Pharaoh on the throne who thought of nothing but the
god Aton, there was practically no government as Egypt
had known it. As a result minor officials seem to have
taken over and, as minor officials are apt to do whether in

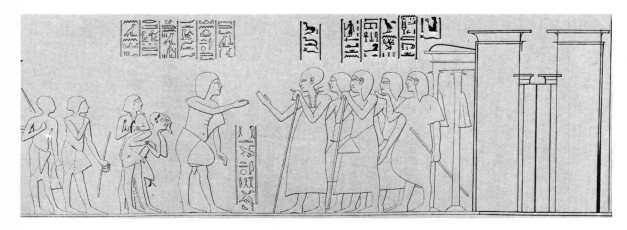

The chief of police of Akhenaton handing over two robbers to the vizier of
Amarna   *(from 'the Rock Tombs of El-Amarna' by N. de G. Davies)*

ancient Egypt or in the world today, they allowed power
to go to their heads. The Egyptian minor officials seem to
have filled their own coffers at the expense of an in-
creasingly embittered populace, while at the same time
robbing their Pharaoh and, through him, the state.

Queen Nefertiti would have known what a deplorable
state the country was in and might have talked things
over with two great confidantes. These were Tey, who
had been what is called 'Her Nurse' but actually must have
been something more like 'Head of the Nurseries'. The
other was Ay, always described as The Divine Father.
Ay after Akhenaton was the most important man in the
state. These two – Tey and Ay – were married and
though probably not royal were highly born and Ay
enormously influential.

It would seem possible at these conferences – if they

took place – that plans were discussed for saving Egypt from certain disaster. One plan may have been for Nefertiti to leave Akhenaton and move to a palace of her own. All the royal family and many of the highly born had palaces all over Egypt which from time to time they would visit. If Nefertiti did move into another palace, probably taking the three youngest daughters with her, it was a palace at the other end of el-Amarna from the one used by Akhenaton. The reason for this move, if it took place, would appear to have been that Nefertiti in a palace of her own would be more free to communicate with Thebes and so soothe the priests of Amun. Perhaps too she believed she might bring hope to her distraught country. But it is equally likely Nefertiti did not move at all but just died in her bed. For the truth is nobody knows much about Nefertiti except from her busts, which show her to have been startlingly beautiful.

Tutankhamen was not, as a little boy, expected to be a Pharaoh for Akhenaton shared his throne with a young man who it is believed was Tutankhamen's older brother. It was naturally supposed this older brother, who was only about twenty-two, would outlive Akhenaton and on his death rule Egypt alone. This did not happen for Akhenaton and his co-ruler died within a few months of each other so Tutankhamen was pronounced heir to the throne.

Tutankhamen was by that time married to Ankhesen-paton. He was probably about six or seven when the marriage took place and she nine or ten. The marriage made Tutankhamen more royal for the princess was very royal indeed. It was not of course a wedding like a grown-up wedding – that would happen some years later. In fact it is unlikely to have made much difference to the children's lives for they would have remained what they had probably always been – playmates, with the princess treating Tutankhamen as a little brother.

Seventy days had to pass between the death of a Pharaoh and the crowning of a new one. This was the period during which the mummifying took place. Those seventy days must have been very busy ones for Tutankhamen, for Ay and for the priests who had to teach him his part in the very elaborate coronation ceremony. Tutankhamen came to the throne when he was probably about nine years old. Though of course he would have understood the importance of becoming not only the Pharaoh but also a god, it is unlikely he had any idea how important Ay, The Divine Father, considered his coronation for he was too young to have grasped how near to shipwreck Akhenaton had brought the country.

There was no question of Tutankhamen being crowned in any other place than Karnak, so that right from the start he re-established the god Amun to the position his priests and most of the country believed to be rightly his.

Probably for some days before his coronation the little boy would have fasted and been through ritual purifications. On the great day itself he made his first appearance

64

Painted ivory plaque from the lid of a coffer showing Tutankhamen and Ankhesenamun in a garden. The lower frieze shows young women plucking mandrakes

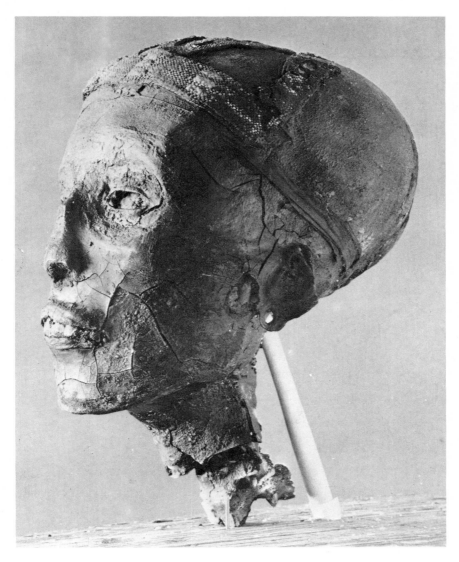

Tutankhamen's mummified head   (Griffith Institute, Ashmolean Museum)

very humbly dressed. He would have been naked to the waist with a simple pleated loin-cloth and he had bare feet. First he would have been led to the great temple of

(a) *The queen brings unguents and flowers to the king*
(b) *The queen fastens a necklace round the king's neck*

Karnak by all the most important people of the land, headed of course by Ay, The Divine Father.

Before the coronation there would have been great efforts made to bring back to Karnak the glories that once were there, but covering up years of neglect is a long job, and no doubt there were still signs of the way Amun had been treated in buildings in need of repair and weeds where once there had been well-kept gardens.

Only the highest officials accompanied Tutankhamen beyond the first courtyard to the temple. When he moved on he found waiting to meet him priests wearing masks of the gods. One, wearing the mask of Horus of the Horizon, which was a falcon's head, took the little boy by one hand and led him behind a screen, while another priest, representing the god Aton, took his other hand. It was then the child performed the first rite before his enthronement.

Next Tutankhamen was taken into the hall of the temple where he was handed over to another group of priests for further purification. For this he had to step into a shallow pool. At the quarters of the pool were four priests representing Thoth, who wore the beak of an ibis, Seth, whose mask had a curved muzzle and erect square ears, falcon-beaked Horus, and the fourth a god called Dunawy who also wore a falcon mask. These four poured purifying liquid over Tutankhamen out of tall gold jugs. This liquid signified divine life, so as soon as it had covered the child he was considered fit to appear before the gods.

The boy was then led to the very holiest part of the building for the actual coronation rites. Here were two temples, one representing the north of Egypt, the other the south. In the first temple were assembled priests each representing one of the most important gods. There they held a ceremony, or what we should call a service, at the climax of which Tutankhamen had to enter the northern temple. In this temple a priestess representing the goddess of the north was waiting for him. Of course Tutankhamen had been carefully trained so he knew what to expect, otherwise he might have found the goddess of the north a bit startling. She represented the royal cobra as seen on the foreheads of Pharaohs, so she was wearing a huge head of a cobra.

Now came the actual crowning. A priest appeared wearing a leopard skin and a wig which finished with a great curl down one side. Aided by other priests this priest placed one after the other the crowns of Egypt on Tutankhamen's small head. The first was a white mitre followed by a red mortar-shaped cap. It is to be supposed a Pharaoh wore no wig during his crowning so the head-dresses could fit snuggly on to his scalp. These first two head-dresses when worn together formed a third head-dress known as 'The two Powerful Ones'. Then he received a special head band, the blue leather crown and, finally, a diadem of two tall plumes, plus various wig covers. Poor little boy, his head must have ached, but all these head-dresses were the insignia of the age-old royalty

Tutankhamen's wig-box (Griffith Institute, Ashmolean Museum)

of Egypt, and each meant something important. All the head-dresses were his in trust until his death, though they were kept in the temple of Karnak and only brought out when needed, just as we keep our royal insignia in the Tower of London until it is required. When Tutankhamen left that chapel he was wearing his blue leather crown and hanging from his belt was the tail of a beast, which some say was a giraffe but which seems more likely to have been a bull. On his feet were special sandals with the names of all the countries Egypt had defeated marked on the soles.

Now came Tutankhamen's enthroning. For this he was led to a shrine carved out of a solid block of rose granite. Kneeling before the shrine the god Amun was supposed to confirm his right to wear the blue leather crown, and the hand of the god was believed to touch the boy's neck.

After this there was a long service which combined in it a great deal of magic. Then, leading the procession, Tutankhamen went outside where the coronation service was performed all over again. This time in public so that everybody could watch the scene.

Head of the king from a coronation group where the god Amun is placing his hand on Tutankhamen's head-dress (Metropolitan Museum of Art, New York)

Either before or after his crowning Tutankhamen, had he been older, would have been expected to show his physical prowess by baiting savage bulls or even wrestling with a lion. Naturally a little boy of nine couldn't do such things, but he probably had to make some ritual gesture showing how brave he would be when he grew older.

In almost all carvings of Pharaohs they carry the crook in one hand and the flail in the other, these were the insignia of Osiris. In Tutankhamen's tomb, as you will see, there were buried with him two flails and two crooks. The one set are full-sized, the other quite small,

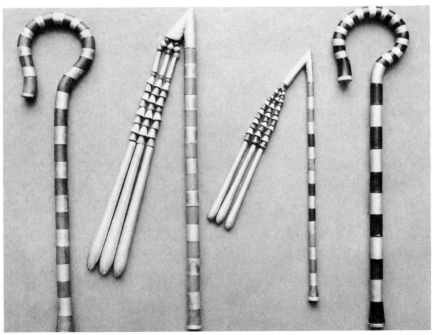

The king's two sets of sceptres: the smaller set bears the name of Aten and the larger the name of Amun   *(Griffith Institute, Ashmolean Museum)*

70

suitable for a small boy to carry, so almost for certain they were used for the first time when he was crowned.

Of course the crowning was not the end of coronation day. For this he travelled by boat through towns and villages full of rejoicing people who had been encouraged to rejoice by a lot of free food and wine. It must indeed have been a glorious day for everybody for it seemed the bad old days were gone, the gods were back in their rightful positions, and they had a new young Pharaoh who was sure to do well, for was he not a son of Amun and had he not got Ay, The Divine Father, to guide him?

6

Tutankhamen reigns

Tutankhamen did not rule for very many years for he died when he was eighteen or nineteen. During his reign a great deal that was good for Egypt happened. It is doubtful how much Tutankhamen himself had to do with the improvements, it is more likely that much of that which was done was suggested to him by Ay, The Divine Father, for, Pharaoh though Tutankhamen was, he was still for much of his reign a schoolboy attending to his lessons.

It is not possible to know who were the important men around Tutankhamen when he was growing up; there was of course Ay, The Divine Father, and a very wise soldier called Horemheb, but the ancient Egyptian custom of surrounding the Pharaoh with the friends with whom he had grown up was not possible in the case of Tutankhamen, for of course in the early part of his reign his friends were still doing lessons with him.

The seventy days between the death of one Pharaoh and the crowning of another was always a strain on the

On the two following pages: Head of the child-king emerging from a lotus flower like the rising sun; found at the entrance of the tomb Head of a couch in the form of the hippopotamus goddess

Drinking cup found at the entrance of the tomb

country. These were the days it took to mummify the last Pharaoh. It must have been a particularly black patch following the death of Akhenaton for he had been feared during his life, so when he was dead the superstititious Egyptians believed that wickedness and disorder were let loose on the country. To add to the people's fears news from abroad was not good. The Syrians were forming a pact with the Hittites, and there was much unrest in Palestine.

In Egypt signs of decay were everywhere. Shrines had been thrown down and often smashed. Paths leading to them were overgrown and weeds sprouted like fields of corn. The priests who, however bad things were, had held the country together had been dismissed and so were scattered. There was in fact a blight over everything for it was believed the gods were offended. Just how bad things were is shown by this translation of what is written on a huge stele which Tutankhamen erected at Karnak. A stele is an upright slab or pillar usually with an inscription written on it.

'Now when His Majesty appeared as King, the temples from one end of the land to the other had fallen into ruin; their shrines were desolate and had become wildernesses overgrown with weeds; their sanctuaries were as though they had never been; their precincts were trodden paths. The land was in confusion for the Gods had forsaken this land.'

Thanks to Ay and other wise men conditions improved

The Boy Pharaoh

A lion dedicated by Tutankhamen in the temple of Soleb
(Trustees of the British Museum)

reasonably soon. Statues of gold were erected to the various gods. Priests were recalled and properly housed and looked after. New priests were created so that people everywhere should know a priest by sight and name. The temples were rebuilt and the slaves, singers and dancers who worked in them were supported from the palace. Aton, god of the sun, was still worshipped but not as the one and only, he was one among the many so his special

74

cult which had caused all the trouble was soon forgotten.

Quite soon after he came to the throne Tutankhamen, with of course his queen Ankhesenpaton, left el-Amarna and went to live in Memphis. This, naturally, meant a general move, for everybody who was anybody packed up and moved too. It must have been sad leaving and boarding up comparatively new houses, but many of the owners took any part of the building worth having with them. At the same time imagine all the moving the scribes had to do, the rolls and rolls of papyrus they had to pack, for of course where the Pharaoh went the records went too. It was quite understandable, seeing the bad name the town had earned, that it was decided to abandon el-Amarna. Not of course that it would be entirely abandoned like a ghost town in an American western, for imagine the covetous eyes of the poor as they watched the rich sail away. It is not known what happened but common sense tells us that squatters would have settled in before many days had passed.

From objects and wall decorations found in Tutankhamen's tomb it would seem that the royal children grew up to be a happily married couple. There is tenderness and love in the way the two are shown together. Some artist must have seen Queen Ankhesenpaton actually fastening a necklace round the King's neck as shown on the gilt shrine.

Although there were of course lessons at the beginning of Tutankhamen's reign and at all times a lot of state

*The panel from the desk-shaped coffer: the king hunting and fishing in
the marshes*   *(Griffith Institute, Ashmolean Museum)*

business it is nice to know there was also fun too, for all
work and no play would have turned him into a dull boy.
One of his tasks as Pharaoh was to visit as much of his
country as possible, so restoring the people's confidence.
So the King and Queen did a lot of travelling from one of
their beautiful palaces to another, and wherever they
went a new statue to a god was built or an old one repaired.
But that Tutankhamen was responsible, probably under

Ay's direction, for so much was not known to posterity. This was because so anxious were those who succeeded him to take credit for what he had done, as well as to cut out of their history what they considered as the disgraceful period of Akhenaton's rule under which Tutankhamen had grown up, that often Tutankhamen's mark on statues, temples and other works of art was obliterated and the mark of Ay or Horemheb, who succeeded Ay, inserted in their place.

All the travelling the children had to do from one palace to another would have been enjoyed by the young King and Queen, but best of all were the revivals of the great religious festivals.

Every year – before the reign of Akhenaton – a most beautiful feast was held in honour of the god Amun. It was called the feast of Opet. Opet was another name for the Luxor temple. From the temple, Amun, his wife Mut and their son Khonsu were supposed to proceed by barges down the Nile. The barges were accompanied by a flotilla led by the royal barge. This festival was revived.

Before the great procession started Tutankhamen performed the first rites at Karnak, sprinkling a libation over flowers and other gifts presented to the gods. Then the procession started to the strains of music, the priests carrying the gods in miniature barges which were to be placed on the great barges. Meanwhile Tutankhamen was borne on a litter to his own barge and, when all was ready, gave the order for the procession to start.

The solar boat on which Tutankhamen is escorting the gods
(*Princetown University Press, Bollingen Series: drawing by Pièrre Clère: A. Piankoff*)

It must have been a glorious sight. The great barges of the gods, and probably Tutankhamen's, would have been gold-plated, glittering under the blue sky and scorching sun. All the barges were towed down the river by sailors who were encouraged to pull hard by musicians and singers. Probably the music was of the sea-shanty type. Of course both banks were packed with onlookers gathered to enjoy a good day out, and they naturally joined in the singing. Almost certainly Tutankhamen enjoyed himself too and sang as loudly as anybody else.

During the outward journey Tutankhamen had to seize an oar and pretend to row his barge. This was to tell everybody that on behalf of his father Amun he was responsible for the journey.

When the procession reached Luxor the barges were tied up, and with deep respect the little model of Amun's barge was carried to his temple. It was a real struggle for his priests to get the little barge to its destination for the

78

people would practically have blocked the way with all their offerings. As well, of course, then as now, a festival means stalls of things for the public to eat and drink. Then there would have been side-shows, dancers, acrobats and tumblers. When at last Amun's procession had entered his temple the real holiday for the people began, and at a guess a pretty good party was had by all.

Eleven days later the procession of barges returned down the river. Before this happened oxen, sent for the occasion by the Nubians, had been sacrificed to make certain the current – which was strong at that season of the year – would bring the procession safely home.

Of course all Tutankhamen's duties as Pharaoh were not as amusing as the feast of Opet but no doubt he did everything that was expected of him under the eye of Ay, The Divine Father. One great occasion shows the importance of foreign affairs during his reign. Tutankhamen had a friend many years older than himself called Huy. He was sent to be viceroy of Nubia, which you remember is where the Sudan is today.

The investiture of Huy was a very grand affair. For this occasion Tutankhamen was very elegantly dressed. He wore a great robe of pleated linen, the blue leather crown and in one hand the crook and flail and in the other the emblem of the sign of life. On his feet were sandals and attached to him a long animal's tail. He sat on his throne under its great canopy.

Then Huy was led in, also very grandly dressed, and

The Investiture of Huy   *(from 'The Tomb of Huy' by Davies and Gardiner)*

carrying a flail. After speeches he was invested with a ring which was the seal of office which gave him the power to rule all Nubia as the representative of Tutankhamen. Huy on his part, among many promises, vowed to send Tutankhamen chiefs from all foreign lands bearing rich gifts.

This ceremony must have been repeated though perhaps more simply many times, for Tutankhamen could not be everywhere and it seems certain his reign was blessedly free from war.

80

Nubian tributes presented to the viceroy *(from 'The Tomb of Huy' by Davies and Gardiner)*

Although Tutankhamen and Ankhesenpaton had a happy though short life together, as in all lives sad things happened as well. Of course as they grew older and loved each other as husband and wife like every other young couple they wanted babies, particularly a baby boy to be Tutankhamen's heir. It was not to be. They did have two babies but both were born dead and both were girls.

Nothing whatsoever is known about the death of Tutankhamen. He could have contracted some illness. If you were really ill in ancient Egypt your chances of recovery must have been slight for, as you know, in spite of the remarkable knowledge they had of the human body through embalming, it does not seem to have been passed on to doctors. Or, of course, he could have been poisoned, but, if so, by whom and what for is anybody's guess. So now we have to go forward again to 1922 and see with Howard Carter and Lord Carnarvon Tutankhamen's tomb and all the marvels it contained.

Before we leave the world of over three thousand years ago there is an interesting story to tell. Nobody has made this up. It really happened. Almost as soon as Tutankhamen was dead Queen Ankhesenpaton, who up to then had been a very royal but shadowy figure whom we know only through portraits of her, started an intrigue. She wrote to the King of the Hittites asking him to send her one of his grown-up sons to be her husband.

Mind you, there was nothing odd about a foreign marriage, one of Ankhesenpaton's sisters had married into a foreign court. No, what is strange is that it seems out of keeping with the date and the pretty girl queen of the portraits. Everything in this book is an attempt to retell what the archaeologists have told us, but here let us have a guess as to what happened. Remember it is only a guess, no knowledgeable person has even hinted at it, yet somehow to this writer it seems not only possible but likely.

It is to be imagined that Tutankhamen knew he was dying. Boys of eighteen do not as a rule drop dead or die in their sleep, so perhaps he had a fatal illness which no doctor knew enough about to cure and so lingered some days. What then more natural than that his loving little Queen should sit on his bed and, probably holding his hand, discuss with him what should happen next?

To Ankhesenpaton it would have been unthinkable that she should share her throne with Ay, The Divine Father, who was not only not royal but old. Their two babies had been born dead so there was no heir. How wise then for Egypt if her Queen could procure a strong young foreign husband. Perhaps it was Tutankhamen who suggested she should write to the Hittite King – nobody

Nobles of the realm drawing the royal catafalque: painting from Tutankhamen's tomb   *('Service des Antiquités de la R.A.U.', Cairo: A. Piankoff)*

knows, but then nobody ever will so our guess is as good as anybody else's.

As it happens, whoever thought up the scheme, it came to nothing. The King of the Hittites first brooded on the letter and then sent somebody to Egypt to find out if it was really sent by Ankhesenpaton. When he found that it was he did send a prince to her, but he never arrived. Perhaps someone murdered him. Soon afterwards Ay was crowned Pharaoh, and from then onwards Ankhesenpaton disappeared from history.

Howard Carter, a born archaeologist so not given to emotion or imagination, when he came to Tutankhamen's last resting-place found himself deeply moved. He wrote: 'But perhaps the most touching by its human simplicity was the tiny wreath of flowers, as it pleased us to think, the last farewell offering of the girl Queen.'

It pleases us too to think of Ankhesenpaton putting that wreath on Tutankhamen's forehead. Three thousand years ago or today sorrow is the same. Tutankhamen was gone and whatever in future happened to his Queen she was bereft. Life from then on would be bleak without him.

7

Opening the tomb

You remember in Chapter 3 we left Howard Carter, having uncovered sixteen steps and a sealed doorway, cabling to to Lord Carnarvon to come out and see what had been discovered. On November 26th 1922, which Howard Carter described as 'the day of days', Lord Carnarvon arrived with his daughter. By this time a descending passage nearly seven feet high filled with rubble was nearly cleared, but was making Howard Carter very anxious for it was obvious people had been there before him. In other words tomb robbers. Was this tomb to prove like so many other tombs to have been so robbed there was nothing left to find? Clearing the passage was a slow job, for they found mixed with the rubble broken pottery, painted vases, jar sealings, heaps of tiny fragments of small articles and some water skins.

All the morning of the 26th the work of clearing the passage went on but still without a sign of another door. Then in the middle of the afternoon thirty feet below the outer door at last a second sealed doorway appeared. The seals, though faint, were clearly recognizable as belonging to Tutankhamen. But here again there were signs of illegal entry for the door had been opened and then closed and replastered. By this time Howard Carter and his helpers were beginning to make up their minds that they must accept they had not found Tutankhamen's tomb. Behind the door there would be a cache possibly of objects of value, but their hopes of a royal tomb were dying.

Slowly – agonizingly slowly – the remains of the rubble was cleared until at last the whole doorway was on view. With hands that trembled Howard Carter made a little opening in the corner of the door. Through this he inserted a testing rod which told him nothing for as far as it could reach it touched nothing. Then, just in case there were foul gases, candles were pushed through. Then Howard Carter widened the hole a little, put in a candle and held it steady.

At first Howard Carter saw nothing for the hot air escaping from the sealed room made the flame flicker. Then by degrees his eyes became accustomed to the light and he could see. And what a sight he saw. Strange animals, statues of gold – gold everywhere, unlimited gold. At first Howard Carter was struck dumb and couldn't speak. Then Lord Carnarvon, bursting with curiosity, asked: 'Can you see anything?' In a daze like someone who has seen a vision Carter answered: 'Yes. Wonderful things.' Then, still in a daze, he widened the hole and put a torch through. This time he beckoned to Lord Carnarvon to join him and together, strangely silent, they stood and stared.

Howard Carter wrote that the first reaction of most archaeologists on stepping into rooms sealed and closed by pious hands centuries before is embarrassment. So many thousands of years have passed since feet have trodden where yours are now treading. Then you get a secondary reaction. The past is not that far away, you look at a bowl half full of mortar left by the door, there is a lamp blackened by smoke, a finger mark on what was then new paint, and a little farewell wreath dropped in the doorway.

Of course the next reaction, so Howard Carter tells us, is the natural one of wild curiosity. What is in those boxes and jars? What joy to break them open and see what is inside. You just try and imagine what Lord Carnarvon and Howard Carter saw by the light of that torch. At first, naturally, it was a confused picture – Aladdin's cave come out of a fairy story into the real world. Then gradually important pieces stood out. There were three great gilt couches carved in the shape of monstrous animals with the animals' heads looking savagely realistic. There were two life-sized figures of Tutankhamen. They were black with golden kilts, sandals and staffs. On their heads were the sacred cobras. These two statues faced each other. Then between these couches and figures were innumerable smaller objects: alabaster vases, exquisitely carved

The two life-size statues of Tutankhamen   (Griffith Institute, Ashmolean Museum)

chairs, a golden throne, over-turned chariots. There was no end to it.

Then suddenly a thought came to the two men. These things at which they were looking were called funerary objects. There was no tomb. No mummy. Was this after all just a cache though of particular magnificence, or was there more, far more, for them to discover? Thinking these things the two men peered round more closely and then they saw it. Between the two black statues of the king there was yet another door. Both men knew at once

88

where that door would lead to. Behind it in all his glory the dead Pharaoh would be lying.

*   *   *   *

Other people's jobs are nearly always fascinating to the outsider. Howard Carter wrote three books about his discoveries in Tutankhamen's tomb and each book shows the reader different aspects of the difficulties confronting archaeologists. The first thing that Howard Carter knew had to be done was to organize efficient lighting so that they could see clearly what objects there really were in the room, which was in future to be known as the ante-chamber.

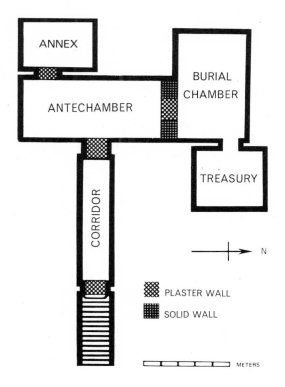

Plan of the tomb and identification of the rooms at the time of the discovery (George Rainbird Ltd)

As soon as powerful lights were set up it became possible to see the immense importance of the discovery, but straight away the lights showed something disappointing. The newly discovered door, before which the two statues of Tutankhamen were standing, was not intact as they had believed, for a small opening had been made at the bottom of the door big enough for a boy or perhaps a dwarf to creep through. This hole had, when finished with, been filled up and resealed. So after all Lord Carnarvon and Howard Carter were not to be the first to enter the burial chamber. Robbers or a robber had been there before them.

Anybody but an archaeologist would have found it almost impossible to resist the temptation to break down the door and see what was on the other side. But archaeologists don't work like that, everything that is done has to be done slowly, carefully and with great delicacy. Another difficulty was that nothing could be moved to make it possible to open the door, for an immensity of work had to be done on each object to make it safe to move it before it could be touched. Then everything must, before moving, be labelled, photographed and catalogued. So it was obvious that many skilled hands and a great deal of time must elapse before the door could be opened. But first there was a most important job to be done, every bit as important as it had been at the time of Tutankhamen's death, and certainly more efficient. The great find must be made safe from robbers.

Howard Carter was very good not only at making

Howard Carter's robber-proof grille　　　*(Griffith Institute, Ashmolean Museum)*

things robber proof but at catching robbers. For this job of sealing the antechamber so that no robbers could get in he measured the doorway for a grille made of thick iron bars. Of course a robber-proof iron-bar grille would take time to make so, for the time being, there was only one thing to do, put back all the rubble and seal up the tomb so that it looked as it had before.

Meanwhile there was intense excitement not only in archaeological circles but all over the world. For without official news the wildest rumours circulated. In the end Lord Carnarvon and Howard Carter decided to have a grand official opening with all the most important people, both Egyptian and British, present and to write a full account of the discovery to *The Times* in London.

Members of the Egyptian Cabinet at the grand official opening of Tutankhamen's tomb   *(Radio Times Hulton Picture Library)*

After this official opening the tomb was closed again and, leaving trustworthy people in charge, Howard Carter went to Cairo to buy what was needed before the objects in the antechamber could be touched. These included all types of photographic material, packing boxes of every size and shape, thirty-two bales of calico, more than a mile of wadding and an equal amount of surgical bandages.

As well, while he was in Cairo, Howard Carter thought about personnel. How many helpers would he need? And what especial skills must each have?

Obviously of first importance was a photographer. Here he was very lucky for with the utmost generosity the Metropolitan Museum New York lent not only a brilliant photographer but other skilled men as well. Help too was available from scientists and archaeologists already in Egypt. As a result on December 25th all was ready. The robber-proof grille was in place. A makeshift dark-room was arranged for the photographer. The method of sorting and marking worked out. Then and only then could Howard Carter give the order to start work on the ante-chamber treasures.

8

The antechamber

The antechamber was a small room roughly twenty feet by twelve feet. This meant only a few could work in it at the same time, and those that did had to tread as delicately as cats, for one hurried careless step would do irreparable damage.

It is not possible in a short book to begin to list even part of what was found; we must just look at a few things so that we can feel why Howard Carter was so excited and see what enormous care had to be taken before anything was handled.

We have to imagine a little box-room into which un-wanted objects have been shoved without any sense of order. Only, instead of the mixture of broken toys, perambulators, sewing-machines, pictures and boxes which are in today's box-rooms, in the antechamber everything was of immense value, often made of gold, which originally had been placed in exact positions with infinite care, but were now strewn, pushed and shoved just any place by robbers snatching at what seemed the most valuable and portable pieces. The photographer took some wonderful pictures of the antechamber as it was when Howard Carter first saw it, and some of these are published in the first volume of his three books. These pictures make one marvel at the patience and skill which brought order out of chaos.

The first object the archaeologists came across was a beautiful wishing-cup. This was made of pure semi-translucent alabaster. Both handles were shaped like lotus flowers, and these supported kneeling figures. It is a glorious vase.

On the right as the workers came in were two funeral bouquets; these were made of leaves, one had fallen over, the other was propped against the wall. In front of the wreaths was something that at first glance Howard Carter realized would prove to be the greatest of the artistic treasures. It was a painted wooden casket completely covered in gesso. Gesso is plaster of Paris or gypsum prepared for use in painting and in sculpture. On to the gesso pictures were painted in beautiful colours. On the lid there were hunting scenes, on the sides battle scenes and on the ends Tutankhamen as a lion trampling on his enemies. But no description can describe the beauty of the casket for the painting and workmanship are indescribably lovely. Nobody knows now what the casket should have contained for in the antechamber the robbers, having ransacked the room in a mad rush, seem to have shoved

One of Tutankhamen's sandals
(Griffith Institute, Ashmolean Museum)

the objects they did not want or could not carry back into the nearest receptacle. On the other hand it could have been the priests in charge of the room who, discovering the robbery, had hurriedly repacked. Anyway the contents of the casket were just a jumble. There were some of Tutankhamen's sandals made of rush or papyrus, and some grander ones worked in gold. There were royal

One of the two life-size statues of the king: black wood with applied gilded plaster

robes covered in beads and sequins and one all over gold rosettes – in all three thousand of them. Amongst other miscellaneous objects a gilt head-rest. All these things just crushed into the casket in a higgledy-piggledy way.

The whole of the west wall of the chamber was taken up by the three couches they had first seen through the hole in the door. Howard Carter had seen wall paintings of such couches but never before the real objects. These three each represented a different animal: the lion or cheetah of which there is a photograph, the cow and a mixed up beast half crocodile, half hippopotamus. Of this too there is a photograph. These couches were made in four pieces so they could be carried easily. The actual bed part fixed to the animal sides by a hook or staple. Above, below and around these couches was a mass of smaller objects.

Howard Carter in the first of his three-volume books (which took him ten years to write) describes some of these objects. A bed made of ebony and woven cord. A collection of most exquisitely decorated arrows, bows and staves; one of these arrows was encased in gold and was a masterpiece of the jeweller's art. One bow had a captive's head at each end so that their necks notched the string. The bloodthirsty idea being that each time Tutankhamen drew his bow he strangled a couple of prisoners. Between the couch and the bed there were four torch-holders, one of which still had its linen wick in place in the oil cup. There was another casket, this one inlaid

The back of the gold-plated throne: the queen Ankhesenamun is putting the finishing touches to the king's toilet

The king's 'camp-bed' as it was found

The king's 'camp-bed' unfolded   *(Griffith Institute, Ashmolean Museum)*

with bright turquoise blue faience which is neither pottery nor porcelain but somewhere in between. This casket, when opened, had exciting things in it. A priest's leopard-skin robe decorated with silver and gold stars and a gilt leopard head, this last inlaid with coloured glass. There was a big splendidly decorated scarab made of gold and lapis lazuli-coloured glass. A buckle cut from sheet gold. And a collection of faience collars and necklaces made in brilliant colours. There was too a collection of large gold rings tied up in a piece of linen. This last turned Howard Carter's mind back to the original robbers. Who else would bundle rings together in that untidy way?

It would take pages to describe even a quarter of the other finds the archaeologists made but one is of especial interest. It is a little chair. It is decorated in ebony, ivory and gold, and could only have been made for a small child to sit in. It must almost certainly have been Tutankhamen's used in his nursery when he was a little boy and now gathered with all his great possessions ready to be with him again when he had finished his journey through the underworld.

Perhaps the most important treasure found in the anteroom was a golden throne. This was discovered by the third couch, the mixed up beast half hippopotamus and half crocodile. It is a lovely throne heavily decorated in glass, stone and faience. It is mounted on long thin legs with lions' paws and is surmounted with lions' heads. The arms are carved serpents wearing crowns and they have wings. The back is supported by bars and between them there are cobras. But the great glory of the throne is the scene on the back panel. This is one of the loveliest and most tender of Tutankhamen and Ankhesenpaton. It shows the Queen putting the finishing touches to Tutankhamen's toilet. In the picture red glass is used for the exposed parts of the bodies of the King and Queen. The crowns are of the brilliant turquoise blue faience as seen on other funerary objects. Both the King and the Queen are dressed in silver. Both are wearing huge jewelled collars and these and other decorations are made of beautifully patterned inlay of coloured glass or faience. The whole background is gold. In the picture the Queen is putting something on Tutankhamen's shoulder, perhaps a drop of scent. But what, apart from its intrinsic value, makes this picture so valuable is what the artist saw. There is love and tenderness in the picture which, over three thousand years later, can make us say 'This boy and girl adored each other'.

Much of the space in the antechamber was taken up by the chariots. There were four of them and they had been taken apart to get them into the antechamber. Probably in the beginning they had been re-assembled after a fashion but the robbers had made a dreadful mess of them as they struggled to tear the gold off them. But robbers were not the only reason for the mess the chariots were in. All the horse trappings, harnesses and the like had been made of leather. Affected by damp this untanned leather had turned into revolting masses of glue. Fortunately even the harnesses were covered in gold so the archaeologists could see that in time they could replace the original leather.

The oddest things were discovered mixed up with the

pieces of chariot. Alabaster jars, baskets, bead sandals and four horse-hair fly-whisks, each with lion heads on the handles which were made of gilded wood.

Altogether in that antechamber there were over six hundred objects. Clearing the chamber of them Howard Carter wrote 'was like playing a gigantic game of spillikins'. For those who do not know, spillikins is a very old game in which sticks of anything from mother-of-pearl to wood are piled together and the players score for each stick they remove, with a little handler, without causing a movement amongst the other sticks.

In the case of the findings in the antechamber moving anything was indeed like spillikins for it was only too easy to plan to take away one object to find it was the holder up of half a dozen or so more, which would then come toppling down. To get over this difficulty all kinds of props were designed so that each object would in time depend upon itself.

Another great difficulty was the condition of the various objects. Some were perfect but others were dangerously frail. For these last it was necessary to decide whether it was possible to move the object where it could be studied under better conditions or whether that would be too dangerous, so it must have preservative treatment on the spot.

To explain the problem Howard Carter described some sandals made of patterned beads. Whatever the beads had been threaded on had long since decayed. As the sandals lay on the floor they looked perfect as if they could be picked up, but try that and what was left was a handful of beads. This was got round by encasing each sandal in melted paraffin wax, so that when the wax hardened anyone could touch it.

Of course special treatment had to be used for the bouquets for without it they would have crumbled into dust. These were made movable by several sprayings with a celluloid solution.

As you can imagine this meant that every single object required different treatment. Think what that meant when there were over six hundred objects to move. Imagine too what it was like to be Howard Carter, who knew that in his charge were objects each of which could tell today's world pages and pages of untold history. Reading Howard Carter's books cannot but give the rest of us, who are not archaeologists, a deep respect for those who are.

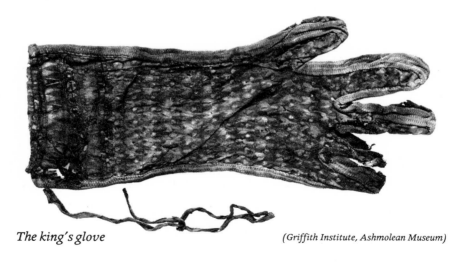

The king's glove (Griffith Institute, Ashmolean Museum)

9

Clearing the antechamber

We already know that Howard Carter was a highly-strung man and that as well he was an exceptionally dedicated one. Imagine then how he felt when, having reached the antechamber full of such marvellous treasures most of which needed the most delicate handling, he found himself thwarted at every turn. What thwarted Howard Carter and his team was people.

Archaeologists are specialists so, like most specialists, they tend to talk about their work only to each other, supposing, usually rightly, that outsiders will not understand or even be particularly interested. But Tutankhamen's tomb had become world news and that meant that the world's national papers required up-to-date information to give their readers, as to what had been found and what was going on, so they rushed to Egypt.

Special correspondents of national newspapers are highly-paid people who expect to give their editors exactly the news they want on the day they want it.

Visitors at the entrance to the tomb (The Times)

So imagine what happened. There were the eager team of archaeologists longing to get on with their work in the tomb. And there were the special correspondents just as eager to get on with their job. To do this they demanded interviews, they glued their eyes to the tomb entrance so as to report everything that they saw and as well they hid, ready to pounce on any member of the archaeological team who might have a bit of special information to pass on. Obviously Howard Carter understood the newspapermen's problem and did what he could to help, but special newspaper correspondents were not all. In those first few days telegrams and then letters poured in on him like a tidal wave. It was the most mixed mail, full of offers of help and, of course, congratulations, but also demands for souvenirs – even for a pinch of desert sand; naturally nobody had time to answer them.

Then there were visitors. In those first days from early in the morning they arrived in hordes, riding on donkeys or in sand-carts or two-horse cabs. They came prepared to spend the day camping out. Above the tomb was a low stone wall, and round and on this wall the visitors made their headquarters. Howard Carter was very conscious of these sightseers and was sorry there was so little for them to see.

Worst of all were visitors who, for one reason or another, had to be shown round the antechamber. These groups, mostly of VIPs, started slowly, but by the end of a week more and more came until work in the antechamber was brought to a halt. In the end, ten days after the opening of the antechamber, the archaeologists decided to clear out. They reburied the tomb, and locked and barred their laboratory. When they returned a week later the tomb remained buried and the laboratory was closed to all visitors.

At the time this was considered very high-handed behaviour and there was a great deal of ill-feeling. But what were the archaeologists to do? Ignorant visitors could do untold damage to objects which, remember, did not belong to the archaeologists. Then there was the time-wasting factor. If everybody who felt they had a right had been shown the finds almost no work would have been done. In fact during the first winter after the finding of the tomb the archaeologists did give the visitors a quarter of their working time, which meant they had to work on into May and May in Egypt is a desperately hot month quite unsuited to meticulous work.

People have wondered why Tutankhamen's tomb caused the furore it did. To understand you must look at your history books. Between 1914 and 1918 the most dreadful war the world has ever known had been fought. Millions of men never returned and those that did filled the world's towns and villages with cripples, constant reminders of the horrors that had been lived through. The aftermath of any war is depressing for everybody, there is so much adjusting to be done. After the 1914 war the papers did not help, being full of conferences and reparations, nothing to lift the heart. Then one day in 1922 there was a splurge of headlines: 'Buried Treasure!' There can be few so dull witted that their eyes do not shine at those words 'Buried Treasure'. Of course everybody wanted to be there, and those who lived too far away wanted to read of the glorious discovery. But, understandable though the public's reaction was, it undoubtedly slowed things up, possibly by years.

Now let us go back to the antechamber and that giant game of spillikins. As we know, the first person needed before clearing could start was the photographer. Lighting had already been fixed, two mobile electric standard lamps each giving out 3,000 candle power light. We know that the Metropolitan Museum of Art in New York had nobly agreed to send an expert photographer. His name was Harry Burton; it is his photographs in volume one of Howard Carter's three books which show so clearly what the antechamber was like when it was first discovered.

It was clear that no object could be touched until it had been photographed so that there was a permanent record of what was found and where. So of course it was necessary for Harry Burton, having taken a photograph, to develop it at once to see it was exactly what was wanted. For this purpose Howard Carter knew of an empty cache tomb near by which Harry Burton was allowed by the Egyptian Government to use as a dark-room. Howard Carter says in one of his books that the sight of Harry Burton sprinting from Tutankhamen's tomb to the cache tomb to develop a photograph was one of the popular pleasures for the sightseers grouped by the wall above the tomb.

What of course Howard Carter was working towards was clearing the antechamber entirely, not only because then the sealed door guarded by the two statues of Tutankhamen could be opened but because, in a laboratory, the objects could be examined under proper conditions.

The obvious way to catalogue the objects was to do so

ABOVE *Bringing treasures from the tomb*
BELOW *Part of the couch is removed from the tomb*

(*Radio Times Hulton Picture Library*)

systematically going round the room, and this indeed was done. But it was clear that quite another system was also needed for it must be possible to group objects together that belonged to each other, and that could not be done systematically for in the muddled state of the antechamber it was likely that some object belonging to a group might be found at the other end of the chamber, which meant its number would not explain where exactly it was found.

It was Harry Burton's camera which solved that problem. Printed numbered cards were placed on every object and at least one photograph was taken of it showing the number. The prints of these numbered objects would be filed with the details about it, so when in the future anyone wanted to know exactly where in the chamber a certain object had been discovered it would show by the number on the photograph.

The next problem was, when ready to move where were all the objects in the chamber to go? There were three main requirements. One, a tremendous amount of space. Two, it must be robber-proof. Three, privacy. The team must be able to work in peace.

In the end they were allowed by the Egyptian Government the use of an empty tomb. It was splendid from the privacy point of view because it was not a tomb visited by tourists, so the path leading to it could be closed.

There was not a great deal of space in the tomb itself, but there was a lot outside on which, as time passed, they built a photographic studio and a carpenter's shop.

To keep out robbers they used a huge steel gate. This had several padlocks so that each head of a department could have a key. These keys were never parted with even to loan to a colleague. The need for this care was because to this day Egypt is full of people willing to buy objects said to be ancient. This means there are plenty of thieves around eager to get hold of such objects. So it was impossible to be too careful. Luckily Howard Carter was smart at circumventing robbers.

Another difficulty that Howard Carter had to overcome was mileage. From Tutankhamen's tomb to Cairo was five hundred miles and in the nineteen-twenties you didn't just hop on an aeroplane as we do today; if anything was needed someone had to go by train. This meant in every department great forethought. For imagine the delay it would have caused if the men in charge of preserving an object ran out of a particular type of preservative. It is very hard for us today to grasp what five hundred miles meant when you had to rely on road or rail transport.

Once arrangements had been made for the storage of the finds the work of clearing the antechamber began to go ahead. Naturally it was painfully slow work but it was systematic. In all seven specialists were used. The first of course was Harry Burton with his camera. When he was satisfied with his photographs two draughtsmen took over. It was their job to draw a scale-plan of the chamber, every object being shown in projection. Then Howard

Carter and his right-hand man called Callender did the first noting, clearing and preparing the objects for removal, and, after removal, two archaeologists waited at the other end to write down details and to mend and preserve.

The first object they removed was the wooden casket already described. It, like every other object, was placed on a padded wooden stretcher to which it was securely fastened by bandages. Enormous numbers of these stretchers and miles of bandages were used because obviously it was seldom that either stretchers or bandages could be used twice. When a stretcher had been delivered to the storage tomb it had to be laid gently down until such time as the specialists could unpack it and decide what needed doing. About once a day a convoy, under heavy guard of course, would leave Tutankhamen's tomb to proceed to the storage tomb. This was of course the high spot of the day for the tourists waiting above. The gossip stopped, knitting was dropped and out came the cameras. Even a procession of stretchers with what is on them covered in bandages is a thrill when you have waited all day for it.

It was the large objects which gave the most trouble, particularly the couches. These had been taken apart at the time of Tutankhamen's burial to get them into the antechamber. Now they had to be taken apart again, and it took five men to do it. Two supported the bed part. Two looked after the animals. The fifth worked underneath

111

The dismantled chariots   (*Griffith Institute, Ashmolean Museum*)

loosening the hooks which naturally, in over three thousand years, had set tight in their bronze staples. When the couches were at last out of the antechamber they were packed in chests which were waiting for them.

Far the worst things to move were the chariots. They had not been placed whole in the antechamber in the first place; then robbers had turned them upside down searching for gold, and over the years the undressed leather of the harnesses had turned to glue. It was an appallingly

Unguent box (?) in the shape of a double cartouche, probably used for ritual purposes

The last object is carried to the storage tomb   (*Radio Times Hulton Picture Library*)

difficult task to get the pieces of chariot out, but it was managed somehow.

Seven weeks after the clearance of the antechamber had started it was finished. Nothing was left, not even one bead. All was gone, that is except for the two life-sized black statues of Tutankhamen who still guarded the as yet unopened sealed door.

Tutankhamen's funeral mask in solid gold inlaid with semi-precious stones and glass-plate

10

Behind the sealed doors

The 17th February 1923 was the day chosen to open the sealed door. Twenty guests were invited for this occasion, which of course included Lord Carnarvon, whose money and enthusiasm had made the discovery possible, and his daughter Lady Evelyn Herbert.

Very careful arrangements had been made for these guests for obviously they must be well out of the way when the tomb was opened. First the two black statues of Tutankhamen had been screened so that they could not be damaged when the door was taken down. Between the statues a little platform had been built for Howard Carter, Mr Callender and others of his staff to work from the top downwards at pulling down the door. From this platform through the anteroom to the passage outside a team was waiting to handle each brick as it was removed from the door. They were to work as people do with buckets when there is a fire to put out and no fire brigade to do it. A short distance from the platform a barrier had been built, and behind this were chairs for the twenty guests. It was lucky they had chairs for as it turned out the opening of the tomb took some hours.

In spite of all the care he had taken for every emergency, Howard Carter, who went alone on to the platform to make the first incision in the door, admits that his hand trembled. Very slowly and carefully he chipped away the plaster and small stones which formed the outer layer of the door. Then after about ten minutes, while it is to be suspected the twenty guests held their breaths, he pushed a torch through a small opening he had made. What he saw made him gasp. Within one yard of the sealed door stretching as far as he could see and completely blocking the way into the chamber was a wall of solid gold.

Now Callender and one other of his staff joined Howard Carter on the platform and together they began to remove the bricks. This proved a difficult job for the bricks were of all different sizes, some appallingly heavy, others quite light. As well the chamber behind the door was about four feet lower than the antechamber so there was great danger of a brick falling forwards. The work was accomplished by Howard Carter easing each stone out with a crowbar, while a second man held it to prevent it falling into the tomb room, then the third man took the stone from them and passed it to the relay team waiting to pass it outside. But one excitement everybody shared. As the door came down they could all see what had looked like a wall of solid gold. They were at the entrance of the true burial chamber of Tutankhamen, and the wall of gold was really the side of an enormous gold shrine which had been built to cover the stone coffin called a sarcophagus.

In all it took two hours before sufficient of the doorway had been removed and it was possible to go through it. Then at the last minute there was a hold up. A bead necklace was discovered lying in the doorway, probably dropped by a robber. Whatever the necklace had been threaded on had long ago disintegrated so every bead had to be picked up separately. Imagine having to pick up beads when you can see ahead of you wonders greater than our world has ever known. However, at last the beads were collected, and holding an electric light on a long lead Lord Carnarvon, Howard Carter and one other entered the burial chamber.

There could be no doubt that it was the burial chamber for, towering over their heads, was the great gilt shrine beneath which Pharaohs were laid. This shrine was so enormous that they discovered it filled almost the entire chamber. The whole of it was covered in gold and the sides were decorated with glorious blue faience magic symbols, repeated over and over again. At the north end of the chamber were stacked the seven oars Tutankhamen was supposed to need to row himself across the waters of the underworld. The walls of the whole chamber had pictures on them painted in vivid colours.

At the eastern end of the shrine they came to folding doors; these were closed and bolted but they were not

Howard Carter examining the doors of one of the gilt shrines
(Radio Times Hulton Picture Library)

sealed. Did that mean that robbers had been there before them? They drew back the bolts and opened the doors. There ahead of them were more folding doors, but on these folding doors the bolts were held by a seal. In any case the three men did not want at that moment to go any further. They knew now without doubt that behind the second sealed doors was the mummified Tutankhamen. A

Pharaoh. So what they all felt was awe, reverence and respect.

Turning away to the far end of the chamber a surprise was waiting for them for there was a third room smaller than the other two. This was called The Treasury. The door to this room was not closed nor sealed so just standing where they were they could see the entire contents. Obviously when so many beautiful objects have been discovered it is hard to say: 'This is the most wonderful.' But what the three men saw in The Treasury made these words possible.

Facing them on the far side of the room was a large shrine-shaped chest completely covered in gold. This was crowned with a decoration of sacred cobras. Around the chest, standing free, were four statues of guardian god-desses. These four golden goddesses, each with her arms held out protectingly, are startlingly moving. One at the back of the shrine and one in front are looking tenderly after their charge. The other two are looking over their shoulders to see no intruder comes in by the door. Look at the frontispiece and you can see for yourself how truly lovely these goddesses are. Without doubt the watching men knew they were looking at the canopic chest. This had to do with mummifying the dead Pharaoh. In it were those parts of his body which would have decayed and so were removed from the head and body before he was mummified.

There were some other wonderful things in The

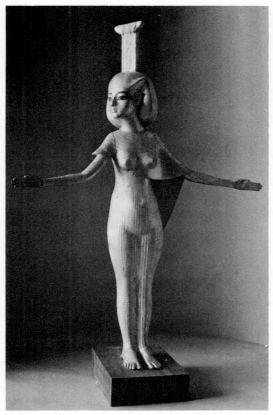

Three of the golden goddesses guarding the shrine-shaped chest
(Griffith Institute, Ashmolean Museum)

Treasury, but it was difficult for the three men to concentrate on them for however hard they tried to focus on other things their eyes were always drawn back to the four guardian goddesses.

All the twenty guests were in time shown round the tomb. Then, three hours after they had come in, hot and dusty they stumbled out to meet the blazing blue Egyptian sky. But they felt changed people. They had seen wonders that no one else in the world had seen. Life would never be quite the same again.

11

The last discovery

Tutankhamen's burial chamber was not opened until 1926. There were many reasons for the delay, Lord Carnarvon's death being probably the greatest. He, you remember, had not only paid for the vast task of uncovering the tomb and repairing and listing the finds, but he had quietly done a lot of work behind the scenes, smoothing things out for Howard Carter. Certain it is that after his death there were continual rows and frictions between the Egyptian authorities and Howard Carter. The trouble was not financial, for Lord Carnarvon's widow was very anxious the work on the tomb should continue at her expense as a memorial to her husband.

Another reason for the delay was that there was so much work still to be done on the objects already found. Apparently in all archaeological work there is great danger in haste, it is impossible to move too carefully. Then the world-wide interest in Tutankhamen had made Howard Carter in great demand as a lecturer. So he undertook a protracted lecture tour which began in America and finished in Madrid.

By January 25th 1925 all troubles and frictions had been smoothed out, and Howard Carter was home from his tour so he and his team were ready to re-open the tomb. But because it was late in the cool season all that was done at that time was to prepare and pack the objects they had already found ready to send to the Cairo Museum. So they decided to leave the tomb itself to the beginning of the next cool season. It was the wish of the Egyptian Government to have the tomb ready to show the public by the next tourist season. Even without being officially opened from January to March 1925, 12,300 tourists came to visit the tomb, and 270 parties to see over the laboratory. So that the archaeologists got any work done at all was a miracle.

In the September of 1925 Howard Carter again set off for Egypt. Everything was planned in advance for, from previous experience, the team knew what they would find. The King's mummy would be in a nest of coffins one inside the other, rather like those wooden Russian dolls which each enclose a smaller doll. This nest of coffins, which would be inside the sarcophagus, would have to be lifted out so each could be treated separately. As things turned out this was a terribly long job not completed until May 1926.

As we know, because the seal on the bolts was intact, no robber had ever opened all the gilt shrines. There

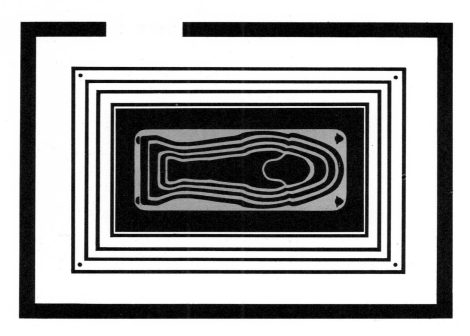

Diagram showing the four golden shrines, the linen veil, the stone sarcophagus and the three mummiform coffins   (George Rainbird Ltd)

were four in all. So, judging by the appearance of Tutankhamen's sarcophagus, the team expected to find the three coffins and Tutankhamen's mummy in perfect condition. But apparently in archaeology you can take nothing for granted, for what they found was everything in an appalling state. The original work had been beautifully done. The body of Tutankhamen was swathed in layer after layer of the finest linen. He was covered from head to foot with ornaments. He was lying in a coffin of pure gold. But it was because such care had been taken that all was in such a deplorable state.

The monarchic animals protecting the neck of the mummy
(Griffith Institute, Ashmolean Museum)

It was part of the burial rites that the body and the coffins should be covered in unguents, which means an ointment used for lubrication. A great quantity of unguents had been used for the burial of Tutankhamen and must have been of a fatty nature though at the time it was used it would have been in liquid condition. But as the years passed the fatty contents had gone bad so it was unfortunate that so much had been used. So when the coffins were opened what was found was everything covered in decayed unguent which had formed a hard pitch-like mass. This meant that the systematic uncovering of the coffins which had been planned was impossible, for the linen bindings in which they were wrapped fell to pieces at a touch.

The Boy Pharaoh

Howard Carter in his preface to the second volume of his three books says: 'Nevertheless, though the undertaking was not such a clean piece of work as one would have wished, I am glad to say little, if any, data was lost, and all the objects were eventually preserved.' There writes the true archaeologist. It might have been disappointing that it was not a clean piece of work but little of any of the data was lost. It might have taken months instead of weeks but it was data that mattered. A true archaeologist is a most dedicated type.

Tutankhamen's sarcophagus was made out of a solid block of yellow quartzite. It was nine feet long, four feet ten inches wide and four feet ten inches high. It is considered now to be one of the finest examples of its kind in the world. One of its great glories is the carving at each end, it is in high relief and is a picture of the four little guardian goddesses.

The next stage was to lift the lid. This proved difficult because the lid was broken. Evidently something had happened at the time of the burial; perhaps the proper lid was not ready. Anyway the one that was on the sarcophagus was cracked.

Whatever the spectators – and there were a lot of them when the sarcophagus was opened – had expected to see, what they saw was a surprise. It was layer after layer of fine linen shrouds. These were rolled back one by one and then the viewers had their reward. This was a golden portrait of the boy Pharaoh and was of glorious workmanship and covered the entire lid of the outermost coffin. On it rested the tiny wreath of flowers which it is likely was placed there by Ankhesenpaton.

Work on raising the nest of coffins did not begin until the next season – 1926. It must be rather like getting a boat ready to go to sea when a huge archaeologist enterprise is started. There is so much to be done and so much careful inspection needed it seems as if the start will never be made. On this occasion Howard Carter was reasonably pleased with conditions in the burial chamber. The insect powder he had put down had kept the tomb free of insects. The sheet of glass he had put over the effigy of Tutankhamen had kept it from harm, now all was ready to raise the lid of the first coffin.

This coffin, like its lid, proved to be a most beautiful piece of work. It showed an effigy of Tutankhamen lying in state. The coffin was inlaid with gold and decorated with cut and engraved glass to look like jasper, lapis lazuli and turquoise.

While all this work was in progress something had been puzzling the team of workers: why were the coffins so enormously heavy? It was when they came to the innermost coffin that they found the answer. The second coffin and the innermost coffin were so tightly wedged together it was not possible to get even a little finger between the two. They were also stuck together with unguent. The unguent was expected, if not in such great quantities, for unguents were obviously an important

Tutankhamen's profile from his funeral mask   (Griffith Institute, Ashmolean Museum)

126

part of the ceremonial burial. Those who have read The Bible will remember that when Christ was in the house of Simon the leper there visited him a woman carrying an alabaster box of ointment of spikenard – very precious. And she broke the box and poured the contents on to Christ's head. Some present when this happened were very shocked, pointing out that the ointment could have been sold for a lot of money. But Jesus understood for he said: 'Let her alone. She hath done what she could: she is come beforehand to anoint my body for the burying.' Though this was said over thirteen hundred years later, that story shows how important the use of unguents was believed to be at a burial.

The work of raising the second coffin from the innermost was a tremendous job. What was needed was great heat to melt the decayed unguent. The innermost coffin was solid so would not melt under great heat but the gold mask, which was a great feature of the second coffin, had to be protected. This was done by covering it in blankets which were continually soaked in water. Next the two coffins were turned upside-down allowing paraffin stoves to throw enormous heat on the black solid mass of the decomposed unguent. After some hours the treatment began to work and it was possible to lift the shell of the second coffin off the innermost one which remained resting on the trestles. No wonder the team had marvelled at the weight of the three coffins for now they knew the answer. The innermost coffin, in which was the mummified body of Tutankhamen, was made of solid gold.

This is really the end of the story of the finding of Tutankhamen's tomb. Everything was eventually cleared from the burial chamber and sent to the Cairo Museum, where those who are lucky enough to visit Egypt can see most of what Howard Carter found. Of course the excitement is not there, but awe and wonder remain. What we are looking at is the possessions and last resting-place of a boy of whom, until Carter's discovery, nobody had heard, but who is now the most famous of all the Pharaohs.

One of the statuettes of Tutankhamen used during the ritual pilgrimages of the funeral
(Griffith Institute, Ashmolean Museum)